# Lecture Notes in Compute

*Commenced Publication in 1973*
Founding and Former Series Editors:
Gerhard Goos, Juris Hartmanis, and Jan van

Anant Madabhushi   Jason Dowling
Pingkun Yan   Aaron Fenster
Purang Abolmaesumi   Nobuhiko Hata (Eds.)

# Prostate Cancer Imaging

## Computer-Aided Diagnosis, Prognosis, and Intervention

International Workshop
Held in Conjunction with MICCAI 2010
Beijing,China, September 24, 2010
Proceedings

 Springer

Volume Editors

Anant Madabhushi
Rutgers University, Piscataway, NJ, USA
E-mail: anantm@rci.rutgers.edu

Jason Dowling
CSIRO Australian e-Health Research Centre, Herston, QLD, Australia
E-mail: jason.dowling@csiro.au

Pingkun Yan
Philips Research North America, Briarcliff Manor, NY, USA
E-mail: pingkun.yan@philips.com

Aaron Fenster
Robarts Research Institute, London, Ontario, Canada
E-mail: afenster@imaging.robarts.ca

Purang Abolmaesumi
University of British Columbia, Vancouver, Canada
E-mail: purang@cs.queensu.ca

Nobuhiko Hata
Brigham and Women's Hospital and Harvard Medical School, Boston, MA, USA
E-mail: hata@bwh.harvard.edu

Library of Congress Control Number: 2010934414


CR Subject Classification (1998): J.3, I.4, H.5.2, I.5, I.2.10, I.3.5


LNCS Sublibrary: SL 6 – Image Processing, Computer Vision, Pattern Recognition,
and Graphics

| | |
|---|---|
| ISSN | 0302-9743 |
| ISBN-10 | 3-642-15988-5 Springer Berlin Heidelberg New York |
| ISBN-13 | 978-3-642-15988-6 Springer Berlin Heidelberg New York |

springer.com

© Springer-Verlag Berlin Heidelberg 2010
Printed in Germany

Typesetting: Camera-ready by author, data conversion by Scientific Publishing Services, Chennai, India
Printed on acid-free paper        06/3180

# Preface

Prostatic adenocarcinoma (CAP) is the second most common malignancy with an estimated 190,000 new cases in the USA in 2010 (Source: American Cancer Society), and is the most frequently diagnosed cancer among men. If CAP is caught early, men have a high, five-year survival rate. Unfortunately there is no standardized image-based screening protocol for early detection of CAP (unlike for breast cancers). In the USA high levels of prostate-specific antigen (PSA) warrant a trans-rectal ultrasound (TRUS) biopsy to enable histologic confirmation of presence or absence of CAP.

With recent rapid developments in multi-parametric radiological imaging techniques (spectroscopy, dynamic contrast enhanced MR imaging, PET, RF ultrasound), some of these functional and metabolic imaging modalities are allowing for definition of high resolution, multi-modal signatures for prostate cancer in vivo. Distinct computational and technological challenges for multi-modal data registration and classification still remain in leveraging this multi-parametric data for directing therapy and optimizing biopsy. Additionally, with the recent advent of whole slide digital scanners, digitized histopathology has become amenable to computerized image analysis. While it is known that outcome of prostate cancer (prognosis) is highly correlated with Gleason grade, pathologists often have difficulty in distinguishing between intermediate Gleason grades from histopathology. Development of computerized image analysis methods for automated Gleason grading and predicting outcome on histopathology have to confront the significant computational challenges associated with working these very large digitized images.

This workshop aims to bring together clinicians, computer scientists, and industrial vendors of prostate cancer imaging equipments to discuss (1) the clinical challenges and open problems, (2) present state-of-the-art research in quantitative image analysis and visualization methods for prostate cancer detection, diagnosis, and prognosis from multi-parametric imaging and digitized histopathology, and (3) advances in image guided interventions for prostate cancer therapy and biopsy. The workshop aims to acquaint clinicians, urologists, radiologists, oncologists, and pathologists on the role that quantitative and automated image analysis can play in prostate cancer diagnosis, prognosis, and treatment and also for imaging scientists to understand the most pressing clinical problems.

This year's workshop hosted two invited talks. The first was on challenges in histopathological imaging and analysis of prostate cancer by Dr. John Tomaszewski, MD, Chair, Department of Pathology, Hospital at the University of Pennsylvania, Philadelphia, PA. The second invited talk was given by Dr. Jurgen J. Fütterer, MD, Dept of Radiology, Radboud University Nijmegen Medical Centre, The Netherlands, who will be speaking about the role of MRI in prostate cancer detection and diagnosis.

A total of 13 papers were received in response to the call for papers for the workshop. Each of the 13 papers underwent a rigorous, double-blinded peer-reviewed evaluation, with each paper being reviewed by a minimum of 2 reviewers. Based on the critiques and evaluations, 11 of the 13 papers were accepted for presentation in the workshop. An additional two invited papers, from two prominent groups working in the areas of prostate cancer diagnosis and prognosis were also received. The papers cover a range of diverse themes, including (a) prostate segmentation, (b) multi-modal prostate registration, and (c) computer-aided diagnosis and classification of prostate cancer. The clinical areas covered included (1) radiology, (2) radiation oncology, (3) digital pathology, and (4) image guided interventions.

July 2010

Anant Madabhushi
Jason Dowling
Pingkun Yan
Aaron Fenster
Purang Abolmaesumi
Nobuhiko Hata

# Organization

## Workshop Organization

### Organizers

| | |
|---|---|
| Anant Madabhushi | Rutgers University |
| Jason Dowling | CSIRO Australian e-Health Research Centre |
| Pingkun Yan | Phillips Research North America |
| Aaron Fenster | Robarts Research Institute |
| Purang Abolmaesumi | University of British Columbia |
| Nobuhiko Hata | Brigham and Womens Hospital |

### Program Committee

| | |
|---|---|
| Olivier Salvado | CSIRO Australian e-Health Research Centre |
| Richard Levinson | CRI |
| Lance Ladic | Siemens Corporate Research |
| Ali Khamene | Siemens Corporate Research |
| Mark Rosen | Hospital at the University of Pennsylvania |
| Dinggang Shen | University of North Carolina, Chapel Hill |
| Gabor Fichtinger | Queens University, Kingston, Ontario |
| Ernest Feleppa | Riverside Research Institute |
| Ameet Jain | Phillips Research North America |

## Sponsorship

The organizers are grateful to Springer for agreeing to publish the proceedings of the workshop in Springer's Lecture Notes in Computer Science (LNCS). The organizers are also thankful to CSIRO Australian e-Health Research Centre and Bioimagene Inc. for sponsoring the workshop. Special thanks also to the MICCAI 2010 workshop chairs (Bram van Ginneken, Yong Fan, Polina Golland, and Tim Salcudean) and to the paper authors for having submitted high quality papers.

# Table of Contents

# Prostate Cancer MR Imaging

Jurgen J. Fütterer

Radboud University Nijmegen Medical Centre, Nijmegen, The Netherlands

# 1 Abstract

With a total of 192,280 new cases predicted for 2009, prostate cancer (PC) now accounts for 25% of all new male cancers diagnosed in the United States [1]. Furthermore, in their lifetime, one in six men will be clinically diagnosed with having PC, although many more men are found to have histological evidence of PC at autopsy [2,3,4]. Presently, approximately 1 in 10 men will die of PC [5,6]. The ever-aging population and wider spread use of the blood prostate-specific antigen (PSA) test [7,8], as well as the tendency to apply lower cut-off levels for this test [9], will further increase the diagnosis of this disease [10].

An elevated PSA level, abnormal changes in PSA level (i.e. PSA dynamics) such as PSA velocity or doubling time, or an abnormal digital rectal examination are biologic indicators signaling an increased risk of PC. With the improvement and wider range of curative therapies, detection and subsequent exact localization of PC have become increasingly important because of their influence on treatment strategy [11,12]. Two such affected treatments are laparoscopic (robotic) radical prostatectomy and intensity-modulated radiation therapy (IMRT) [13]. The urologists inability to palpate the operating field during laparoscopic surgery makes it even more crucial to know where the cancer is located. Similarly, the urologist must know whether the cancer is near a neurovascular bundle since this affects the decision of whether or not to perform nerve-sparing prostatectomy [14]. IMRT also necessitates accurate PC localization. While giving a standard dose to the prostate, a higher (i.e. boost) dose can be given to any dominant intraprostatic lesion(s) since it is those lesion that regularly appear to be the sites of recurrent disease [15]. Furthermore, precision radiation dosimetry will decrease radiation complications, particularly rectal wall toxicity [16], thereby likely diminishing the development of post-radiation rectal cancer [17].In order to determine the optimal treatment for the individual patient, it is necessary to evaluate all patient and cancer characteristics. Most often used for this purpose are laboratory values (PSA level and dynamics), the results of the digital rectal examination (clinical staging), and histopathologic prostatic biopsy findings (Gleason score). However, MR imaging may play an important role in detecting and localizing areas most reflective of the actual aggressiveness of the cancer. This directly influences the assessment of the patient and may lead to important changes in treatment strategy, which can mean the difference between treatment success and failure.

A. Madabhushi et al. (Eds.): Prostate Cancer Imaging 2010, LNCS 6367, pp. 1–3, 2010.
© Springer-Verlag Berlin Heidelberg 2010

In the mid 1980s, the first prostate magnetic resonance (MR) imaging examinations were performed. Since that time MR imaging has evolved from a promising technique into a mature imaging modality for prostate cancer imaging [18,19]. Beside anatomical information, MR imaging can also provide functional tissue characteristic information. Multi-parametric MR imaging consists of a combination of anatomic T2-weighted imaging and functional MR imaging techniques such as dynamic contrast-enhanced MR Imaging (DCE-MRI), diffusion weighted imaging (DWI), and 1H MR-Spectroscopic Imaging (MRSI). Within a multi-parametric MR imaging examination the relative value of its component techniques, differ. In addition to T2 weighted MR imaging which mainly assesses anatomy, MRSI [20] can add specificity for prostate cancer detection, while DCE-MRI [21] and DWI [22] are both very sensitive and very specific.

The clinical challenges in the work-up of patients with either suspected or proven prostate cancer include detection, localization, TNM-staging, determination of cancer aggressiveness, follow-up of patients in active surveillance protocols, and the determination of the site and extent of cancer recurrence after therapy. In this presentation, the prostate MR anatomy and the basic MR techniques which can be applied in prostate cancer, will be described and the clinical role of MR imaging will be discussed. Finally, three clinically applicable protocols are suggested.

# References

1. Jemal, A., Siegel, R., Ward, E., Hao, Y., Xu, J., Thun, M.J.: Cancer Statistics, 2009. CA Cancer J. Clin. 59(4), 225–249 (2009)
2. Carter, H.B., Piantadosi, S., Isaacs, J.T.: Clinical evidence for and implications of the multistep development of prostate cancer. J. Urol. 143(4), 742–746 (1990)
3. Parkin, D.M., Bray, F.I., Devesa, S.S.: Cancer burden in the year 2000. the global picture. Eur J Cancer 37(suppl. 8), S4–S66 (2001)
4. Konety, B., Bird, V., Deorah, S., Dahmoush, L.: Comparison of the incidence of latent prostate cancer detected at autopsy before and after the prostate specific antigen era. The Journal of Urology 174(5), 1785–1788 (2005)
5. Crawford, E.D.: Epidemiology of prostate cancer. Urology 62(6 suppl. 1), 3–12 (2003)
6. Stewart, S.L., King, J.B., Thompson, T.D., Friedman, C., Wingo, P.A.: Cancer mortality surveillance–united states, 1990-2000. MMWR Surveill Summ 53(3), 1–108 (2004)
7. Catalona, W.J., Loeb, S., Han, M.: Viewpoint: expanding prostate cancer screening. Ann. Intern. Med. 144(6), 441–443 (2006)
8. Hoffman, R.M.: Viewpoint: limiting prostate cancer screening. Ann. Intern. Med. 144(6), 438–440 (2006)
9. Graif, T., Loeb, S., Roehl, K.A., Gashti, S.N., Griffin, C., Yu, X., Catalona, W.J.: Under diagnosis and over diagnosis of prostate cancer. J. Urol. 178(1), 88–92 (2007)
10. Max, W., Rice, D.P., Sung, H.Y., Michel, M., Breuer, W., Zhang, X.: The economic burden of prostate cancer, california, 1998. Cancer 94(11), 2906–2913 (2002)
11. Mangar, S.A., Huddart, R.A., Parker, C.C., Dearnaley, D.P., Khoo, V.S., Horwich, A.: Technological advances in radiotherapy for the treatment of localised prostate cancer. Eur. J. cancer 41(6), 908–921 (2005)

12. Meraney, A.M., Haese, A., Palisaar, J., Graefen, M., Steuber, T., Huland, H., Klein, E.A.: Surgical management of prostate cancer: advances based on a rational approach to the data. Eur. J. Cancer 41(6), 888–907 (2005)
13. Bucci, M.K., Bevan, A., Roach III, M.: Advances in radiation therapy: conventional to 3d, to imrt, to 4d, and beyond. CA Cancer J. Clin. 55(2), 117–134 (2005)
14. Hricak, H., Wang, L., Wei, D.C., Coakley, F.V., Akin, O., Reuter, V.E., Gonen, M., Kattan, M.W., Onyebuchi, C.N., Scardino, P.T.: The role of preoperative endorectal magnetic resonance imaging in the decision regarding whether to preserve or resect neurovascular bundles during radical retropubic prostatectomy. Cancer 100(12), 2655–2663 (2004)
15. Cellini, N., Morganti, A.G., Mattiucci, G.C., Valentini, V., Leone, M., Luzi, S., Manfredi, R., Dinapoli, N., Digesu, C., Smaniotto, D.: Analysis of intraprostatic failures in patients treated with hormonal therapy and radiotherapy: implications for conformal therapy planning. Int. J. Radiat. Oncol. Biol. Phys. 53(3), 595–599 (2002)
16. Roach, M.: Reducing the toxicity associated with the use of radiotherapy in men with localized prostate cancer. Urologic Clinics of North America 31(2), 353–366 (2004)
17. Baxter, N.N., Tepper, J.E., Durham, S.B., Rothenberger, D.A., Virnig, B.A.: Increased risk of rectal cancer after prostate radiation: a population-based study. Gastroenterology 128(4), 819–824 (2005)
18. Steyn, J.H., Smith, F.W.: Nuclear magnetic resonance imaging of the prostate. Br. J. Urol. 54(6), 726–728 (1982)
19. Hricak, H., Williams, R.D., Spring, D.B., Moon Jr., K.L., Hedgcock, M.W., Watson, R.A., Crooks, L.E.: Anatomy and pathology of the male pelvis by magnetic resonance imaging. AJR Am. J. Roentgenol. 141(6), 1101–1110 (1983)
20. Villeirs, G.M., Oosterlinck, W., Vanherreweghe, E., De Meerleer, G.O.: A qualitative approach to combined magnetic resonance imaging and spectroscopy in the diagnosis of prostate cancer. Eur. J. Radiol. 73(2), 352–356 (2010)
21. Tanimoto, A., Nakashima, J., Kohno, H., Shinmoto, H., Kuribayashi, S.: Prostate cancer screening: the clinical value of diffusion-weighted imaging and dynamic mr imaging in combination with t2-weighted imaging. J. Magn. Reson. Imaging 25(1), 146–152 (2007)
22. Scheenen, T.W., Klomp, D.W., Roll, S.A., Futterer, J.J., Barentsz, J.O., Heerschap, A.: Fast acquisition-weighted three-dimensional proton mr spectroscopic imaging of the human prostate. Magn. Reson. Med. 52(1), 80–88 (2004)

# Computer Aided Detection of Prostate Cancer Using T2, DWI and DCE MRI: Methods and Clinical Applications

Henkjan Huisman[1], Pieter Vos, Geert Litjens,
Thomas Hambrock, and Jelle Barentsz

Diagnostic Image Analysis Group, Dept. Radiology
Radboud University Nijmegen Medical Centre,
Nijmegen, The Netherlands
h.huisman@rad.umcn.nl
http://www.diagnijmegen.nl

**Abstract.** One in 10 men will be diagnosed with prostate cancer during their life. PSA screening in combination with MR is likely to save lifes at low biopsy and overtreatment rates. Computer Aided Diagnosis for prostate MR will become mandatory in a high volume screening application. This paper presents an overview including our recent work in this area. It includes screening MR setup, quantitative imaging features, prostate segmentation, and pattern recognition.

**Keywords:** computer aided diagnosis, prostate cancer, segmentation, pattern recognition, screening.

## 1   Introduction

Prostate cancer is the most commonly diagnosed cancer among men and remains the second leading cause of cancer death in men. In 2009, approximately 192,000 in the United States (US) and 9600 in the Netherlands (NL) men were diagnosed with prostate cancer, and 27,000 (US) and 2400 (NL) men died from this disease [20] and (http://www.cbs.nl). The prostate specific antigen (PSA) blood test disseminated 20 years ago, and helped shift the disease stage at the time of diagnosis to a much lower and potentially more curable stage. However, early detection of prostate cancer remains a source of uncertainty and controversy.[20]

Recently, it has been established that PSA and systematic transrectal ultrasound (TRUS) testing can reduce prostate cancer mortality. In a large intention to screen trial, Schroder et al [12] showed a mortality reduction of 20% (improved trial showed 30% [11]). The Schroder clinical workflow had two major problems: low specificity of the PSA test and biopsy as subsequent gold standard. The results showed that 1410 men would need to be screened and 48 cases of prostate cancer need to be treated to prevent one death from prostate cancer.

Magnetic resonance imaging (MRI) can be used to increase specificity, guide biopsy, and improve staging. Prostate MRI has evolved since its first application

A. Madabhushi et al. (Eds.): Prostate Cancer Imaging 2010, LNCS 6367, pp. 4–14, 2010.

in the late 80's [4]. This millennium saw the start of high resolution 3D T2 weighted sequences and 3D dynamic contrast enhanced MR (DCEMR), later followed by 3D diffusion weighted imaging (DWI). Localization of prostate cancer can be performed at a high diagnostic accuracy and has been applied in a first clinical application: MR guided intensity modulated radiotherapy planning [1,7]. Tanimoto et al. [14] using a combination of T2 weighted, DWI, and DCEMR concluded that in patients with a PSA level over 4 ng/ml unnecessary biopsy can be avoided without missing prostate cancer. A recent development is to perform MR guided biopsy of MR determined tumor suspicious regions after having a positive MR. This approach proved to be an accurate method to detect clinically significant prostate cancer in men with repeat negative biopsies and increased PSA levels.[2]

Computer aided diagnostic tools will become essential if mass application of MR would becomes a viable option. Reporting the huge volume of prostate MR accurately and efficient will require skills and the right tools including computerized analysis techniques that help to reduce oversight and interpretation errors. In this paper we describe some of our efforts and recent development on computer aided diagnosis applied to prostate MR.

## 2   Role of MR in Screening

In the Netherlands 2400 men die each year of prostate cancer. In the population 50-80 yr (2.000.000) that would amount to an incidence of aggressive prostate cancer of about 0.1%, where aggresive is defined as lifethreatening. Similar to breast cancer (same order of incidence), screening by repeat testing can find a substantial number of these 0.1% that require treatment at a stage where cure is still possible. It is essential for screening not to inflict unnescessary harm to men without aggressive cancer, therefore a high specificity of the screening test is essential. In contrast to breast cancer, there is a high incidence of non agressive prostate cancer: most men die with prostate cancer, but not from prostate cancer. These non-aggressive cancers do not require treatment and it is thus important to discriminate agressive from non-agressive cancers.

The PSA test alone is not suitable for screening due to its low specificity. At a PSA threshold of 4 [ng/ml] the sensitivity is 51% at a specificity of 91% for detecting aggressive cancers. At a PSA threshold of 3, the sensitivity is 68% at a specificity of 85% [20]. A PSA level of 3 in a group of 10.000 men with on average 10 aggressive cancers would result in about 7 cancers to be correctly found. The same PSA test however will also be positive for 1500 men. In the current workflow (see figure 1) this would mean 1500 unnescessary biopsies. The biopsy is a second test to find the 7 cancers requiring treatment. Regular systematic first session biopsies have a sensitivity in between 60 to 70%. Moreover, biopsy has only 50 to 70 % accuracy to predict true GS in prostatectomy. It is obvious that aggressive cancers will be missed and over- and undertreatment will result.

We are currently investigating means to reduce the number of unnecessary biopsies and increase the diagnostic yield of the biopsies by using MR as a second test after PSA testing. Early results show that MR can operate at a sensitivity of 95% with a specificity of 74% [14]. At that setting about 1100 (74% of 1500) unnecessary biopsies can be avoided. Moreover, the MR can guide the biopsy resulting in more representative and fewer cores [2]. The huge reduction in number of biopsies may render prostate MRI cost-effective. Further research should focus on higher specificity MRI and augmenting TRUS to include MR as guidance using automatical, fast and accurate techniques, e.g. [5].

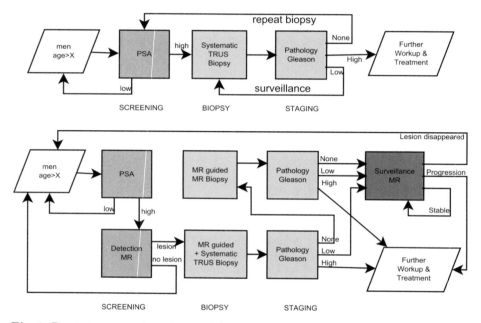

**Fig. 1.** Prostate cancer detection workflows. Top workflow represents the current situation. The bottom workflow is our proposed future situation including MR.

## 3     Quantitative Image Features

Diagnostic imaging and computer aided diagnosis require discriminative image features (or biomarkers) that significantly differentiate (aggressive) prostate cancer from other physiological changes. The raw MR sequences often require further processing to reduce for example the coil sensitivity profile or dependencies on administered contrast agent profile. In this section we focus on our recent work on three types of image features: proton relaxation, diffusion weighted imaging and pharmacokinetic DCE-MRI.

### 3.1     T1 and T2 Relaxation

Quantification of T1 and/or T2 relaxation can be done on the MR machine with dedicated sequences. These sequences are often time consuming, consequently producing either low resolution or are being too slow for practical use in prostate MR. We have been using the method by Hittmair et al.[3] in dynamic contrast enhanced MR to quantify tracer concentration. It uses an additional proton density weighted MR sequence that adds only a minute to the total acquisition time. The method also produces T1 estimates (or R1=1/T1, see paper appendix). The original method was setup using FLASH sequences assuming a gradient echo signal model. We have extended the method to handle any sequence model. T1 relaxation is a good biomarker to identify recent biopsy locations because hemorrhages resemble malignancy due to the strong and fast contrast enhancement. We use it as one of the features in our CAD systems [18], but we also display T1 images to the clinician.

T2 estimation seemed feasible as well with the above method. As prostate MR includes one or more T2 weighted images. we generalized the Hittmair method further to estimate T2 from a T2 weighted and a proton density sequence and known sequence models [17]. The T2 weighted and the proton density turbo spin echo sequence signals at voxel position $x$ are modelled by:

$$s_{t2w}(x) = G_{t2w}sin(\theta_{t2w})\rho(x)exp(-TE/T2(x)) \qquad (1)$$

$$s_{pd}(x) = G_{pd}sin(\theta_{pd})\rho(x) \qquad (2)$$

where $G$ represents the gain setting and $\theta$ the flip angle and $\rho$ is a function comprising proton density fluctuations and coil profile at location $x$. The $T2$ at position $x$ is then derived by rewriting the above equation to:

$$T2(x) = \frac{-TE}{log(s_{t2w}(x)) - log(s_{pd}(x)) - log(\eta_{t2w,pd})}, \qquad (3)$$

where $\eta_{t2w,pd}$ is the gain ratio estimated using a per patient reference fat tissue with know relaxation properties. The additional effort in that work was to also compensate for movement and deformation of the prostate in between the 15 minutes of the two sequences. The estimated T2 was validated by assessing its diagnostic accuracy. The area under the ROC curve for discriminating benign and malignant lesions was 0.64 for the unprocessed T2 weighted images and 0.86 for our T2 estimate. Further validation with additional T2 estimator sequences showed very good correlation (r=0.97).

### 3.2 Diffusion Weighted Imaging

Diffusion Weighted Imaging (DWI) uses sequences that are sensitive to changes in random Brownian motion properties of water molecules (diffusion) in tissue. The degree of restriction to water diffusion in biologic tissue is inversely correlated to tissue cellularity and the integrity of cell membranes. Quantitative analysis can be made using the apparent diffusion coefficient (ADC) derived from several DWI images at different b strengths. The clinical role of DWI in tumor localization with the prostate has extensively been reported before.

We have established that prostate cancer Gleason Score (GS) is strongly correlated with ADC[2]. We have also established that a normalized ADC value

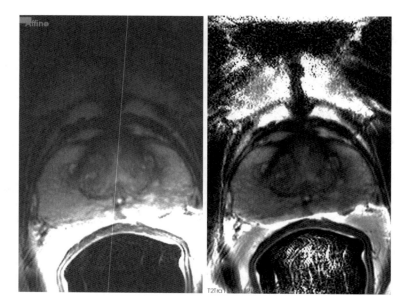

**Fig. 2.** Example images to demonstrate the effectiveness of the T2 estimation method. To the left a slice from the original T2 weighted images, to the right the T2 estimate of the same slice. The coil profile in the prostate has clearly reduced allowing more narrow window settings and show more contrast. Notice the contrast difference of a hypo dense lesion in the left periferal zone of the prostate (arrow).

(using both surrounding and mirror normal PZ) is even stronger correlated to tumor aggressivity. We hypothesize that either ADC is also dependent on normal prostatic tissue physiology and that normal values vary significantly per patient, or ADC is still dependent on MR machine settings that differ per patient.

### 3.3   Pharmacokinetic DCEMR

Pharmacokinetic (PK) MR features quantify blood flow, permeability and tissue extracellular volume. The volume transfer constant $K^{trans}[min^{-1}]$ under permeability limited conditions quantifies the permeability surface area of tissue vasculature and is the most diagnostic feature [1]. Various PK estimation methods exist, generally assuming a two compartment tissue model [15]. We have investigated robust and fast DCEMR curve fitting methods [6] and later on extended this to pharmacokinetic modeling [7] integrated with a reference tissue method [9] to estimate the arterial input function (AIF). The AIF drives the tissue model and directly affects the output. We have established that AIF estimation strongly affects the diagnostic accuracy of PK methods [16]. In a CAD application the common population based AIF achieved an AUC of 0.65 whereas the reference tissue method achieved 0.80. In that same publication we presented an automatic method to segment the reference tissue region.

# 4    Computer Aided Detection

Computer aided detection (CAD) is commonly used in breast cancer screening
to help reduce errors in oversight and interpretation. CAD systems generally
follow a radiologist perception strategy. Within the organ region a quick scan is
performed that results in several initial findings. Each of these findings is further
investigated and if any finding is then above a threshold of suspiciousness the
person is recalled for further diagnostic work-up. The initial voxel based detector
and the lesion classifier are both pattern recognition systems trained on sufficient
annotated cases with validated ground truth.

## 4.1    Prostate Segmentation

Segmentation of the prostate is required to reduce false positives in computer
aided detection of malignant lesions. Segmentation is challenging due to the heterogeneity of the zonal anatomy and embedding in variable context. The prostate
is situated in between bladder, rectum, two levator ani muscles, fat, neuro vascular bundles, pelvic bone and penis. Single object segmentation strategies that do
not account for this heterogeneous context of the prostate (e.g. region growing,
deformable surface models) are unlikely to produce satisfactory results. A first
context based method was published by Klein et al.[8]. They applied atlas based
segmentation on MR to automatically delineate the prostate in a radiotherapy
planning application. They showed good results on the majority of cases. However, the population variation was such that the atlas based population model
could not segment all the cases robustly. Furthermore, their method was rather
computationally expensive, which would be a problem for large scale application.

   We propose a new parametric multi-object probabilistic anatomy model based
prostate segmentation method that incorporates context using a population
model. The pelvic anatomy and modality appearance are modeled by a set of
synthetic parametric anatomy objects. Each object has several parameters to
define shape and appearance. The complete pelvic model is characterized by a
parameter vector $x$. A population based probability function $p(x)$ is defined that
returns the probability of a pelvic model realization to occur in a population.
The pelvic model is fitted to the MR images by finding the optimal set of parameters $x_{opt}$ that maximize the appearance correlation and probability in the
population. The appearance correlation is computed by simulating pelvic MR
images and correlate these with the actual MR images. The population model
constrains the pelvic model parameters to feasible solutions within the population. The population model not only constrains individual anatomical objects
to be within a certain range (e.g. prostate diameter between 2-6cm), but also
captures the contextual relation between objects (rectum is beneath prostate).
The optimal pelvic model is then used to segment the images by probabilistic
modeling. Each anatomic object defines a spatial and grey value likelihood. For
each voxel the likelihood is computed for each anatomical object which is based
on position and grey value(s). The segmentation then results by assigning the
most likely anatomic object label to each voxel.

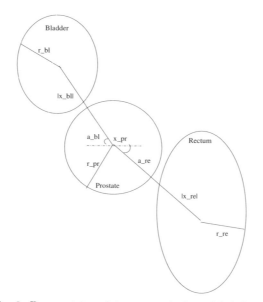

**Fig. 3.** Parametric pelvic anatomical model definition

Estimating the population model function would require large training databases for even modest pelvic anatomy models. We propose a solution to redefine the anatomy model such that context is captured in several parameters and that these parameters are independent. For example, the prostate and rectum center location stored individually requires 6 parameters, none of which individually captures the distance between the two (context). A redefinition of parameters such that the rectum position is defined by a distance from and angle to the prostate captures context, and also renders the parameters reasonably uncorrelated. We have redefined the above pelvic model parameters to $x'$ (see also Figure 3). Assuming independence the population probability function can be redefined as a multiplication of Gaussians $\mathcal{N}$:

$$p(x') = \prod \mathcal{N}_i \qquad (4)$$

Each parameter (i) of the rewritten pelvic model is characterized by a mean and standard deviation. This can be estimated from even a modest training set. Moreover, it allows integration of explicit prior knowledge. For example, prostate size is on forehand known to be within a certain range. Similarly are the grey value distribution of the appearance of several anatomic objects. Figure 4 shows an example segmentation achieved by this method.

## 4.2   Initial Detector

Our first prototype initial detector [19] used a multi-scale Hessian matrix blob detection filter [10] applied to the ADC map. Peak (local maxima) coordinate

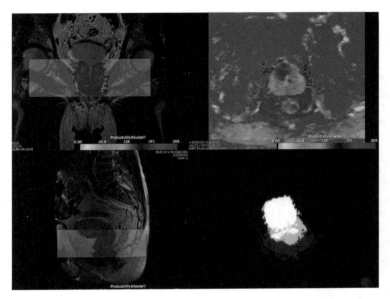

**Fig. 4.** An example pelvic segmentation using our multi object anatomical model. The pelvic model comprised prostate, rectum, bladder and a other class.

detection within a 5 mm region is performed to localize suspicious findings that serve as input to the lesion characterization stage. In the mean time the data set comprises 216 clinical patients scheduled between January and December 2009 that had elevated PSA levels (mean 14ng/ml range:1-58) and one negative biopsy. Histopathology confirmed the presence of PCa in 43 patients. The detection method currently has a sensitivity of 64% at a 6 false positives per patient.

Currently we are working on a multi-feature detection system, using a voxel based Support Vector Machine classifier in conjunction with a lesion based classifier. Examples of voxel features are DCE MRI based features like Ktrans and ve, diffusion based values like ADC and blobness outputs.

### 4.3   Lesion Characterization

For lesion characterization we compute several region based features and classify these with a trained SVM classifier. Several region based tumor features exploit the heterogeneity of a malignant lesion. Similar to breast MR hotspot analysis determines the malignancy of a lesion by its most aggressive part. A robust, simple method is to use region quartiles. One of our best features is the 3rd quartile of Ktrans in a region [18]. A potentially improved hot spot analysis method currently researched for application in breast MR is Mean-Shift cluster analysis [13].

In addition we are also developing an automatic suspicious region segmentation system to segment the region. We use a custom cost function in combination with a LBFGSb optimization method to segment the suspicious region. The cost function is a combination of a population based model and an appearance model.

$$\arg \min_{\boldsymbol{x}} f(x) = p(\boldsymbol{x}) + a(\boldsymbol{x}) \tag{5}$$

Here $p(\boldsymbol{x})$ represents the population model and $a(\boldsymbol{x})$ the appearance model. Also $f(\boldsymbol{x})$ is the complete cost function and $\boldsymbol{x}$ is a set of parameters that is optimized. An example of a parameter that appears in the population model is the radius of the lesion. We assume a normal distribution on the radius, because we know what lesion sizes we can expect in a clinical setting. An example of a parameter in the appearance model can be the mean ADC, because we know that lesions often have a lower ADC value.

After segmentation a number of feature can be extracted from the segmented region, like volume, principle components, mean values and quartiles of quantitative features. These are fed into a trained SVM classifier, after which a probably per region is obtained. This way the false positives we obtain from the voxel classifier can be further reduced.

## 5    Discussion

Screening using prostate MR can be cost effective in screening due to biopsy reduction. The high volume of imaging requires CAD to assist clinicians in fast and accurate reporting. We developed one of the first fully automatic computer aided detection systems for prostate cancer detection on MR. We have shown good results with quantitative features obtained using robust, automatic and dedicated methods. An automated segmentation method of the prostate has been developed that is robust, fast and sufficiently accurate for application in CAD. We are currently exploring further improvements and setting up observer experiments to validate the CAD methods.

## References

1. Fütterer, J.J., Heijmink, S.W.T.P.J., Scheenen, T.W.J., Veltman, J., Huisman, H.J., Vos, P., Hulsbergen-Van de Kaa, C.A., Witjes, J.A., Krabbe, P.F.M., Heerschap, A., Barentsz, J.O.: Prostate cancer localization with dynamic contrast-enhanced MR imaging and proton MR spectroscopic imaging. Radiology 241(2), 449–458 (2006)
2. Hambrock, T., Somford, D.M., Hoeks, C., Bouwense, S.A.W., Huisman, H., Yakar, D., van Oort, I.M., Witjes, J.A., Fütterer, J.J., Barentsz, J.O.: Magnetic resonance imaging guided prostate biopsy in men with repeat negative biopsies and increased prostate specific antigen. J. Urol. 183(2), 520–527 (2010)
3. Hittmair, K., Gomiscek, G., Langenberger, K., Recht, M., Imhof, H., Kramer, J.: Method for the quantitative assessment of contrast agent uptake in dynamic contrast-enhanced MRI. Magn. Reson. Med. 31(5), 567–571 (1994)
4. Hricak, H., Dooms, G.C., McNeal, J.E., Mark, A.S., Marotti, M., Avallone, A., Pelzer, M., Proctor, E.C., Tanagho, E.A.: MR imaging of the prostate gland: normal anatomy. AJR Am. J. Roentgenol. 148(1), 51–58 (1987)

5. Hu, Y., et al.: Mr to ultrasound image registration for guiding prostate biopsy and interventions. Med. Image Comput. Comput. Assist. Interv. 12(Pt 1), 787–794 (2009)
6. Huisman, H.J., Engelbrecht, M.R., Barentsz, J.O.: Accurate estimation of pharmacokinetic contrast-enhanced dynamic MRI parameters of the prostate. Journal of Magnetic Resonance Imaging 13(4), 607–614 (2001)
7. Huisman, H.J., Fütterer, J.J., van Lin, E.N.J.T., Welmers, A., Scheenen, T.W.J., van Dalen, J.A., Visser, A.G., Witjes, J.A., Barentsz, J.O.: Prostate cancer: precision of integrating functional MR imaging with radiation therapy treatment by using fiducial gold markers. Radiology 236(1), 311–317 (2005)
8. Klein, S., van der Heide, U.A., Lips, I.M., van Vulpen, M., Staring, M., Pluim, J.P.W.: Automatic segmentation of the prostate in 3D MR images by atlas matching using localized mutual information. Medical Physics 35(4), 1407–1417 (2008)
9. Kovar, D.A., Lewis, M., Karczmar, G.S.: A new method for imaging perfusion and contrast extraction fraction: input functions derived from reference tissues. J. Magn. Reson. Imaging 8(5), 1126–1134 (1998)
10. Li, Q., Sone, S., Doi, K.: Selective enhancement filters for nodules, vessels, and airway walls in two- and three-dimensional CT scans. Medical Physics 30(8), 2040–2051 (2003)
11. Roobol, M.J., Steyerberg, E.W., Kranse, R., Wolters, T., van den Bergh, R.C.N., Bangma, C.H., Schröder, F.H.: A risk-based strategy improves prostate-specific antigen-driven detection of prostate cancer. Eur. Urol. 57(1), 79–85 (2010)
12. Schröder, F.H., Hugosson, J., Roobol, M.J., Tammela, T.L.J., Ciatto, S., Nelen, V., Kwiatkowski, M., Lujan, M., Lilja, H., Zappa, M., Denis, L.J., Recker, F., Berenguer, A., Mttnen, L., Bangma, C.H., Aus, G., Villers, A., Rebillard, X., van der Kwast, T., Blijenberg, B.G., Moss, S.M., de Koning, H.J., Auvinen, A., E. R. S. P. C. Investigators: Screening and prostate-cancer mortality in a randomized european study. N. Engl. J. Med. 360(13), 1320–1328 (2009)
13. Stoutjesdijk, M.J., Veltman, J., Huisman, H., Karssemeijer, N., Barentsz, J.O., Blickman, J.G., Boetes, C.: Automated analysis of contrast enhancement in breast MRI lesions using mean shift clustering for ROI selection. Journal of Magnetic Resonance Imaging 26(3), 606–614 (2007)
14. Tanimoto, A., Nakashima, J., Kohno, H., Shinmoto, H., Kuribayashi, S.: Prostate cancer screening: the clinical value of diffusion-weighted imaging and dynamic MR imaging in combination with T2-weighted imaging. J. Magn. Reson. Imaging. 25(1), 146–152 (2007)
15. Tofts, P.S., Brix, G., Buckley, D.L., Evelhoch, J.L., Henderson, E., Knopp, M.V., Larsson, H.B., Lee, T.Y., Mayr, N.A., Parker, G.J., Port, R.E., Taylor, J., Weisskoff, R.M.: Estimating kinetic parameters from dynamic contrast-enhanced T(1)-weighted MRI of a diffusable tracer: standardized quantities and symbols. J. Magn. Reson. Imaging 10(3), 223–232 (1999)
16. Vos, P.C., Hambrock, T., Barentsz, J.O., Huisman, H.J.: Automated calibration for computerized analysis of prostate lesions using pharmacokinetic magnetic resonance images. In: Yang, G.-Z., Hawkes, D., Rueckert, D., Noble, A., Taylor, C. (eds.) MICCAI 2009. LNCS, vol. 5762, pp. 836–843. Springer, Heidelberg (2009)
17. Vos, P.C., Hambrock, T., Barenstz, J.O., Huisman, H.J.: Computer-assisted analysis of peripheral zone prostate lesions using T2-weighted and dynamic contrast enhanced T1-weighted MRI. Physics in Medicine and Biology 55(6), 1719–1734 (2010)

18. Vos, P.C., Hambrock, T., Hulsbergen van de Kaa, C.A., Fütterer, J.J., Barentsz, J.O., Huisman, H.J.: Computerized analysis of prostate lesions in the peripheral zone using dynamic contrast enhanced MRI. Medical Physics 35(3), 888–899 (2008)
19. Vos, P.C., Hambrock, T., Barentsz, J., Huisman, H.J.: Computer-aided detection of prostate lesions at diffusion-weighted mr using a dedicated hessian matrix-based detection scheme. In: Annual Meeting of the Radiological Society of North America (2009)
20. Wolf, A.M.D., Wender, R.C., Etzioni, R.B., Thompson, I.M., D'Amico, A.V., Volk, R.J., Brooks, D.D., Dash, C., Guessous, I., Andrews, K., DeSantis, C., Smith, R.A., American Cancer Society Prostate Cancer Advisory Committee: American cancer society guideline for the early detection of prostate cancer: update 2010. CA Cancer J. Clin. 60(2), 70–98 (2010)

# Prostate Cancer Segmentation Using Multispectral Random Walks

Yusuf Artan[1], Masoom A. Haider[2], and Imam Samil Yetik[1]

[1] Medical Imaging Research Center
Illinois Institute of Technology, Chicago, IL, USA
[2] Joint Department of Medical Imaging, University Health Network
Mount Sinai Hospital, Toronto, Ontario, Canada

**Abstract.** Several studies have shown the advantages of multispectral magnetic resonance imaging (MRI) as a noninvasive imaging technique for prostate cancer localization. However, a large proportion of these studies are with human readers. There is a significant inter and intra-observer variability for human readers, and it is substantially difficult for humans to analyze the large dataset of multispectral MRI. To solve these problems a few studies were proposed for fully automated cancer localization in the past. However, fully automated methods are highly sensitive to parameter selection and often may not produce desirable segmentation results. In this paper, we present a semi-supervised segmentation algorithm by extending a graph based semi-supervised random walker algorithm to perform prostate cancer segmentation with multispectral MRI. Unlike classical random walker which can be applied only to dataset of single type of MRI, we develop a new method that can be applied to multispectral images. We prove the effectiveness of the proposed method by presenting the qualitative and quantitative results of multispectral MRI datasets acquired from 10 biopsy-confirmed cancer patients. Our results demonstrate that the multispectral MRI noticeably increases the sensitivity and jakkard measures of prostate cancer localization compared to single MR images; 0.71 sensitivity and 0.56 jakkard for multispectral images compared to 0.51 sensitivity and 0.44 jakkard for single MR image based segmentation.

## 1   Introduction

Prostate cancer is one of the most frequently diagnosed malignancy in US male population. Recent cancer studies estimate that 220,000 men will be diagnosed and 32,000 will die of prostate cancer in 2010 [1]. Fortunately, the survival rate is very high for the early diagnosed patients. Traditionally, transrectal ultrasound image (TRUS) guided biopsy samples are taken from suspected regions, and pathologists confirm the presence or absence of cancer in the obtained cores. However, cancer may be missed due to the limited number of biopsy samples and

A. Madabhushi et al. (Eds.): Prostate Cancer Imaging 2010, LNCS 6367, pp. 15–24, 2010.

low resolution of TRUS, leading to delayed diagnosis (and thus delayed treatment) of the disease. Accurate image guidance is extremely useful in ensuring that the tissue is collected from suspicious regions for cancer. Hence, investigation of imaging methods to detect these regions is an active research area. *In vivo* imaging can also be used to guide surgery, threapy, and monitor disease progression. Applications of various diagnostic imaging techniques as well as their clinical value in prostate cancer detection, localization and surveillance are discussed in details [2].

As an alternative to TRUS, magnetic resonance imaging (MRI) has been used to localize prostate cancer with varying degrees of success over the past years. Many researchers investigated methods to boost the performance of prostate cancer localization using MRI [3]-[4]. One way of boosting localization performance is to use other MR imaging techniques such as diffusion weighted imaging (DWI) and dynamic contrast-enhanced (DCE) MRI in addition to T2-weighted images. For instance, in [3]-[4], the combination of morphological and metabolic information for localizing cancer are investigated. Combining T2-weighted images with DWI and dynamic contrast-enhanced MR imaging has also produced considerable improvement in prostate cancer localization compared to the classical T2-weighted MRI [5].

Although several studies have been performed with human observers using multispectral MRI; only a few methods were proposed to automatically localize prostate cancer with multispectral MRI [6]-[10]. There is a significant inter and intra-observer variability for human readers, and it is difficult for humans to analyze multiple image datasets motivating the need for automated methods.

On the other hand, fully automated methods are highly sensitive to parameter selection and often do not produce desirable segmentation results. Recently, semi-supervised image segmentation algorithms have been gaining increasing popularity due to their superior performance, efficiency, and ease of application [11], [12]. There are various types of semi-supervised segmentation algorithms present in the literature including Intelligent Scissors, Active Contours, Random Walker [11]. This study is focused on the semi-supervised learning of the third type, namely (seed-based) Random Walker (RW) algorithm. Given an input image and a set of seed points, RW computes the first arrival probability that a RW starting at an unlabeled pixel first reaches one of the labeled seeds, then that unlabeled pixel takes the label with maximum probability.

The main contribution of this paper is the development of a semi-supervised multispectral segmentation framework using random walker by optimally combining images coming from different spectrums or modalities to perform prostate cancer segmentation. Our paper is the first to develop a semi-supervised random walker algorithm with multispectral images, whereas most earlier approaches to multispectral prostate MR image segmentation has considered fully supervised learning techniques and semi-supervised methods are applicable to only images of single type (modality or spectrum).

## 2   Methodology

### 2.1   Multispectral Random Walker

Semi-supervised learning utilizes a few pixels of labeled data coming from the human reader in addition to unlabeled image data to improve the tumor segmentation accuracy. Random walker (RW) algorithm is a graph based seeded segmentation technique that formulates the classical segmentation problem in terms of a discrete (combinatorial) dirichlet problem [11].

A graph can be defined as $G = (V, E)$ with vertices $v_i \in V$ and edges $E = \{e_{ij} = (v_i, v_j) | v_i, v_j \in V, i \neq j\}$. All the edges are undirected and each edge $e_{ij}$ is a weight values $w_{ij}$ standing for the likelihood that a random walker move along that edge. The degree of a vertex is defined as $d_i = \sum_j w_{ij}$ for all edges $e_{ij}$ incident on $v_i$. Given a weighted graph, a set of marked (labeled) nodes $F \subset V$, and a set of unmarked nodes $B \subset V$, such that $F \bigcup B = V$ and $F \bigcap B = \emptyset$, objective is to label each node $v_i \in B$ with a label from the set $K = \{l_1, l_2, \ldots, l_k\}$. Random walker algorithm assigns to each unlabeled node the *first arrival* probability $P(v_i)$ that a random walker starting from that node first reaches a marked node with label $l_s$. The segmentation is then completed by assigning each free node the label with the highest probability [11].

RW algorithm is typically formulated for segmentation tasks with single images. In the case of multispectral prostate MR images, rather than applying RW on each image separately and combining binary segmentation results in an *ad hoc* manner, we develop a method that determines a mathematically optimum set of *image weights* $\boldsymbol{\alpha} = (\alpha_1, \alpha_2, \ldots, \alpha_N)$ that are used for each of the features, where $N$ denotes the number of features of the multispectral image. This weighted combination of features produces a fused image that yields improved RW segmentation for the given set of seeds. Edge weight, $w_{ij}$, for the multispectral problem now becomes

$$w_{ij} = \exp\left\{-\beta\left(\sum_{k=1}^{N} \alpha_k(q_{ki} - q_{kj})\right)\right\}, \tag{1}$$

where $q_{ki}$ indicates the image intensity at $i^{th}$ pixel for image type $k$. Our main objective now is to determine the optimal $\alpha_1, \alpha_2, \ldots, \alpha_N$ values that would yield the minimum cost of Eq. (2), resulting in the optimum segmentation in RW sense. In this case, our cost function can be written as follows,

$$E^{mf} = \sum_{e_{ij} \in E} w_{ij}(P(v_i) - P(v_j))^2 = PL^{mf}P$$

$$\text{st.} \quad P(v) = 1 \quad \text{for} \quad v \in F$$
$$P(v) = 0 \quad \text{for} \quad v \in B, \tag{2}$$

where $L^{mf}$ denotes the laplacian matrix of the fused image, which is a symmetric positive semidefinite matrix. This cost function has two groups of unknowns unlike classical random walker formulation: $\boldsymbol{\alpha}$ and $P(\cdot)$ of unknown pixels $v_i \in B$.

We determine the minimum of this cost function in an alternating fashion for these two groups;

- for a set of $P(\cdot)$, find optimum $\boldsymbol{\alpha}$.
- for a set of $\boldsymbol{\alpha}$, find optimum $P(\cdot)$.

Our final energy function is a function of the *image weights* ($\boldsymbol{\alpha}$) only, since the unknown $P(\cdot)$ is eliminated by substituting its closed form solution given $\boldsymbol{\alpha}$ as shown in Eq. (3)

$$P = \begin{bmatrix} P_{v_F} \\ -L_B^{mf^{-1}}(K^{mf})^T P_{v_F} \end{bmatrix}, \tag{3}$$

where $L_B^{mf}$ and $K^{mf}$ denote the marked and unmarked subblocks of $L^{mf}$ matrix [11]. The $\boldsymbol{\alpha}$ that minimize the energy function in Eq. (2) do not have a closed form expression since the $L^{mf}$ matrix are nonlinearly dependent on the unknown $\boldsymbol{\alpha}$. Therefore, we employ numerical methods to find the $\boldsymbol{\alpha}$ that minimizes this cost function. In this study, we resort to multi-start gradient based algorithms. Multi-start algorithm performs gradient based optimization over a small set of grid points, where each grid point represent $\boldsymbol{\alpha}$ value. Once $\boldsymbol{\alpha}$ is determined, unknown $P(\cdot)$ values can be found by minimizing Eq. (2) yielding the segmentation result.

In our study, we perform the optimization using a nonlinear conjugate gradient method (CGM) to obtain the *image weights* that would minimize $E^{mf}$. Note the CGM does not guarantee convergence to global optimum for our cost function and has a few parameters such as the step size that needs to be selected by *a priori*. Using a small initial step size is a common practice, and the optimum step size is approximated by doubling the step size until the cost function increases or number of iterations exceed a preassigned max-number of iterations, at which point the step size is fixed, and the update is performed.

**Algorithm Summary:**
To summarize, the steps of the proposed algorithm are:

1. Given a set of prostate multispectral MR images, human reader places a pair of seeds on the tumor and normal regions.
2. Initialize multiple sets of $\boldsymbol{\alpha} = (\alpha_1, \ldots, \alpha_N)$ parameters.
3. For each of these $\boldsymbol{\alpha}$, perform the following
   - Using Eq. (1), map the image intensities to edge weights in the lattice.
   - Search for optimum $\boldsymbol{\alpha}$ values using CGM based algorithm.
   - Solve Eq. (2) to determine the random walker probability values and compute cost.
4. Set *image weights* $\boldsymbol{\alpha}$ corresponding to minimum cost.
5. Compute $P(\cdot)$ corresponding to this set of $\boldsymbol{\alpha}$.
6. Obtain the final segmentation by assigning the corresponding label to each node $v_i$.

The parameters $\alpha_i$ essentially produces a fused image that would reduce the cost of Eq. (2), which in general results in a better segmentation result than using any single spectrum image alone or combining multiple spectrums in an *ad hoc* and suboptimal manner as explained in next section.

## 3  Experiments and Results

### 3.1  Description of Multispectral MRI Data

In this study, multispectral MR images are obtained from 10 biopsy-confirmed prostate cancer patients. Axial-oblique fast spin-echo (FSE) T2-weighted, echo planar DWI, multi-echo FSE, and DCE-MRI were acquired before surgery using a 1.5-T MRI system (Echospeed or Excite HD; GE Healthcare, Milwaukee, WI) with a 4-channel phased-array surface coil coupled to an endorectal coil (MEDRAD, Warrendale, PA). All data were obtained with the image plane perpendicular to the rectal wall/prostate interface. Median time between imaging and surgery was 33 days (range 1-129 days).

Acquisition parameters were:

- T2-weighted MRI: TR/TE = 6550/101.5 ms; 320x256 matrix; echo-train length (ETL) = 16; bandwidth (BW) = 20.83 kHz; number of excitations (NEX) = 3; field of view (FOV) = 14 cm; no phase wrap.
- DWI: TR/TE = 4000/77 ms; 128x256 matrix; ETL = 144; BW = 166.7 kHz; NEX = 10; FOV = 14 cm; b = 0, 600 s/mm2. Multi-echo FSE images were acquired at ten echo times (9.0-90.0 ms, in 9 ms increments) for T2 mapping (TR = 2000 ms; 256x128 matrix; ETL = 10; BW = 31.25 kHz; NEX = 1; FOV = 20 cm).
- Datasets for DCE MRI consisted of T1-mapping from multi-slice, multi-flip fast spoiled gradient echo images (FSPGR) (flip-angles: 2, 5, 10, 20; TR/TE = 8.5/4.2 ms; 256x128 matrix; ETL = 8; BW = 31.25 kHz; NEX = 1; FOV = 20 cm), followed by 50 phases of multi-slice FSPGR MRI (flip-angle = 20; TR/TE = 4.3/1.9 ms; 256x128 matrix; BW = 62.5 kHz; NEX = 0.5; FOV = 20 cm; temporal resolution = 10s). Two phases were acquired before injection of 20 ml contrast agent (gadopentate dimeglumine (Magnevist; Bayer Schering Pharma, Berlin, Germany)) at a rate of 4 ml/s, followed by a 20 ml saline flush using a power injector (MEDRAD Spectris MR injection system).

The available MRI dataset consists of several functional, anatomical, and parametric image types; based on preliminary feature selection analysis, we restrict our attention to three types of images (i) T2-maps, ii) ADC, iii) T1-PC (principal component) that have information from three main groups (T2, DWI, and DCE-MRI). T2 maps are calculated from a series of echo time measurements and eliminate the fluctuations in signal intensity as a function of proximity to the endorectal coil seen in T2-weighted, as well as providing quantitative values. Apparent diffusion coefficient maps are derived from DWI parametric maps, and several recent studies [7], [3] have shown the usefulness of ADC maps for localizing prostate cancer. Dynamic contrast-enhanced MRI is a well-known method for detecting and quantifying tumor angiogenesis. Prostate carcinomas can be visualized with axial T1 MR sequences. In this study, we used principal components analysis to derive an image (T1-PC) from the dynamic series instead of using a compartmental model, since parametric images obtained from compartmental models are extremely noisy.

Prostate cancer MR images are notorious for speckle for noise and low signal to noise ratio issues, and therefore denoising is a crucial step. In [12], [13], anisotropic filtering is used to reduce the amount of noise in the multispectral MRI data, which increases the segmentation performance considerably. Similarly, in this study, anisotropic filtering is applied on normalized T2, ADC, T1-PC images data to facilitate the segmentation of tumor nodules. The prostate consists of various zones such as transition zone (TZ) and peripheral zone (PZ). However, in this study we have considered only the PZ region is since 70 % of the prostate cancer occurs in this region [14].

**Ground Truth:** In order to evaluate the effectiveness of the proposed method accurately, ground truth for tumor segments are obtained based on pathology. Upon the completion of radical prostatectomy, the extracted prostate was placed in formalin for 24 hours and embedded in HistOmer gel prior to *ex vivo* MRI. T2-weighted (T2w) images were taken at a 5$^o$ intervals and the angle corresponding to the plane of *in vivo* imaging was determined. The gel-embedded prostate was cut into regular 3mm sections using a rotary blade, along the angle plane determined during the *ex vivo* imaging sessions. For all sections, standard pathological techniques are used to prepare hemotoxylin and eosin (H & E) stained whole mount histologic slides. The whole mount sections are assessed by a pathologists and region of tumor was outlined as ground truth. Then, this tumor location is transferred to the *in vivo* MRI by an expert radiologist, who views *in vivo* MRI, histological slide, and the *ex vivo* MRI of this histological slide. A digitalized histologic section of a patient is shown in Figure 1.(e) from the same patient and location with *in vivo* MR images shown in Figure 1.(a)-(d).

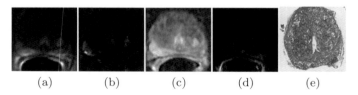

(a)          (b)          (c)          (d)          (e)

**Fig. 1.** An example of multispectral MR images and histological slide. (a) T2-weighted MRI, (b) T2 maps, (c) ADC, (d) T1-PC, (e) digitized whole mount H&E histological slide.

## 3.2   Quantitative Evaluation

A set of pixel-based evaluation criteria are used to assess the performance of segmentation, namely jakkard, sensitivity and specificity. Jakkard measure is an often used a quantitative metric in medical analysis; $jakkard(A, B) = \frac{|A \cap B|}{|A \cup B|}$ where $A$ is the segmentation result and $B$ is the ground truth. Sensitivity is fraction of tumor region that is correctly detected by the algorithm as such, and specificity is fraction in the true segmented healthy region that is also correctly identified.

Fisher's exact test [15] is used to measure the statistical significance of the results (differences in jakkard measure in our case). P-value with Fisher's test provides the probability of obtaining a test statistic at least as extreme as the one that was actually observed. Lower p-values indicate a less likely, thus a more significant result. A p-value of less than or equal to 5 % is typically deemed statistically significant.

For comparison purposes, in addition to our proposed method, we have also implemented the random walker algorithm for the single image spectrums (types) and the average image computed as follows

$$\text{Average} = \frac{q_1 + \cdots + q_N}{N}. \tag{4}$$

In this way, the advantage of the proposed method that optimally combines multiple spectrums will be more apparent, compared to an *ad hoc* combination of spectrums. In our study, we use two average images, namely $\text{Average}_2$ and $\text{Average}_3$. $\text{Average}_2$ is the average of T2 maps and ADC, and $\text{Average}_3$ is obtained by equally weighting T2, ADC and T1-PC considering appropriate signs.

## 3.3   Results and Discussion

First, we anisotropically filter T2, ADC, and T1-PC images as explained in Section 3.1, and user assigns two seed points (one tumor, one normal) on the image. In our analysis, we use only two seeds to make the seed selection easy for the human reader. Using these seed points and a fixed $\beta$ value in Eq. (1), we compute the $P(\cdot)$ values of unlabeled pixels. In our analysis, only the PZ region is considered since 70 % of the prostate cancer occurs in this region. Figure 2 illustrates the random walker segmentation results using single images, average images and the proposed method. These visual results show that the proposed method yields improved segmentation performance. For patient 1 in Figure 2, T2 maps yield the best segmentation performance among single images, and proposed method automatically assigns a higher weight to T2 image and achieves a similar segmentation as seen on the last column. On the other hand, for patient 2 in Figure 2, ADC segmentation performs better than the other image types, proposed method is again able perform improved segmentation and similarly for third example patient.

In addition to visual evaluation demonstrated in Figure 2, Table 1 quantitatively presents the mean and standard deviation the sensitivity, specificity and jakkard measures of 10 biopsy-proven patients. Sensitivity and jakkard measures of proposed method (0.71 and 0.56) are significantly higher than single and average images with similar specificity. Table 2 provides the corresponding p-values for jakkard values of Table 1. As evident by p-values, our method yields significantly improved performance for T2 and T1-PC based segmentation results,

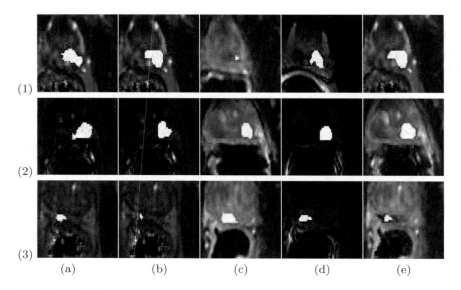

**Fig. 2.** Part a) Ground truth for tumor. Segmentation results (white) using b) T2 maps, c) ADC, d) T1-PC, and e) proposed.

**Table 1.** mean±std of sensitivity/specificity & jakkard random walker (RW) segmentation with T2 maps, ADC, T1-PC, Ave$_2$, Ave$_3$, and proposed

| measure | T2 | ADC | T1-PC | Ave$_2$ | Ave$_3$ | Proposed |
|---|---|---|---|---|---|---|
| Sens. | $0.56 \pm 0.28$ | $0.51 \pm 0.21$ | $0.44 \pm 0.25$ | $0.55 \pm 0.23$ | $0.58 \pm 0.16$ | $0.71 \pm 0.12$ |
| Spec. | $0.94 \pm 0.06$ | $0.98 \pm 0.04$ | $0.98 \pm 0.02$ | $0.97 \pm 0.04$ | $0.98 \pm 0.02$ | $0.95 \pm 0.05$ |
| Jakkard | $0.41 \pm 0.20$ | $0.44 \pm 0.19$ | $0.37 \pm 0.17$ | $0.44 \pm 0.16$ | $0.50 \pm 0.09$ | $0.56 \pm 0.10$ |

**Table 2.** P-value for jakkard measures between pairs of alternating methods using prostate multispectral MRI dataset

| | T2 - Proposed | ADC - Proposed | T1-PCA - Proposed | Ave$_2$ - Proposed | Ave$_3$ - Proposed |
|---|---|---|---|---|---|
| p-val | 0.0107 | 0.0898 | 0.001 | 0.0547 | 0.1719 |

and in some cases p-values does not show statistical significance due to possibly limited number of patients. Notice that our method improves segmentation performance compared to *ad hoc* Average$_2$ and Average$_3$ images as well. In addition, we observe that Average$_3$ segmentation is more accurate than Average$_2$ segmentation which demonstrates the usefulness of including T1-PC images in our analysis.

A disadvantage of the proposed method is the increased computational time required for optimization as expected since multiple images are used for segmentation instead of a single image. Random walker solution is traditionally obtained by solving large, sparse linear system of equations, and there exists many methods for efficiently solving linear sparse systems. For the purposes of this study, we used a multi-start conjugate gradient algorithm on a sparse grid. In future studies, our investigations will mainly focus on decreasing this computation time and also on automated seed selection techniques.

## 4 Conclusion

RW algorithm has been ubiquitously applied to datasets of various image types. However, segmentation methods with RW are applicable only to single image types (spectrums, modality, and intensity) to this date. In this study, we have developed a RW based method that can be used with multispectral MR images. It was shown that the proposed multispectral Random Walker using gradient based optimization algorithm yields improved segmentation performance. The effectiveness of the proposed method is demonstrated by presenting quantitative, statistical and visual results with multispectral MRI datasets acquired from 10 biopsy-confirmed cancer patients. Tables 1 depict that the multispectral MRI noticeably increases the sensitivity and jakkard measures of prostate cancer localization compared to single MR images from 0.71 sensitivity and 0.56 jakkard to 0.51 sensitivity and 0.44 jakkard. Statistical significance of improvements shown in Table 2 illustrates the superiority of the proposed method over the others. Our results have also illustrated the benefit of including T1-PC image in addition to T2 and ADC. Average$_3$ image performed significantly better than Average$_2$ image, motivating the need for dynamic sequences. Compared to the earlier fully supervised methods, proposed method drastically increases the sensitivity while not significantly effecting specificity. In the future, we plan to automate the seed selection process such that process becomes fully automated.

## References

1. American Cancer Society, Surveillance and Health Policy Research (2010)
2. Futterer, J.J., Barentsz, J., Heijmink, S.: Imaging Modalities for Prostate Cancer. Expert Rev. Anticancer Ther. 9(7), 923–937 (2009)
3. Haider, M., van der Kwast, T.H., et al.: Combined T2-weighted and diffusion weighted MRI for Localization of Prostate Cancer. J. of Roent. 189, 323–328 (2007)
4. Futterer, J.J., Heijmink, S., et al.: Prostate Cancer Localization with DCE MR imaging and Proton MR Spectroscopic Imaging. Radiology 241, 449–458 (2006)
5. Yoshikazo, T., Wada, A., Hayashi, T., et al.: Usefulness of Diffusion-Weighted Imaging and Dynamic Contrast enhanced Magnetic Resonance Imaging in the Diagnosis of Prostate Transition-Zone Cancer. Acta Radiologica 10, 1208–1213 (2008)
6. Chan, I., Wells, W., Mulkern, R.V., Haker, S., Zhang, J., Zou, K.H., Maier, S.E., Tempany, C.M.: Detection of prostate cancer by integration of line-scan diffusion, T2-mapping and T2-weighted magnetic resonance imaging; a multichannel statistical classifier. Med. Phys. 30(9), 2390–2398 (2003)
7. Liu, X., Yetik, I.S., et al.: Prostate Cancer Segmentation with Simultaneous Estimation of the MRF Parameters and the Class. IEEE Transactions on Medical Imaging 28(6), 906–915 (2009)

8. Madabhushi, A., Shi, J., Rosen, M., Feldman, M., Tomaszweski, J.: Graph Embedding for Improving Supervised Classification & Novel Class Detection: Prostate Cancer. In: Duncan, J.S., Gerig, G. (eds.) MICCAI 2005. LNCS, vol. 3749, pp. 729–737. Springer, Heidelberg (2005)
9. Ozer, S., Yetik, I.S., et al.: Supervised and Unsupervised Methods for Prostate Cancer Localization with Multispectral MRI. Medical Physics, 1873–1883 (2010)
10. Artan, Y., Yetik, I.S., et al.: Prostate Cancer Localization with Multispectral MRI using cost-sensitive Support Vector Machines and Conditional Random Fields. IEEE Trans. on Image Processing 19(9) (2010)
11. Grady, L.: Random Walks for Image Segmentation. IEEE Transactions on PAMI 28(11), 1–17 (2006)
12. Artan, Y., Haider, M.A., Langer, D.L., Yetik, I.S.: Semi-Supervised Prostate Cancer Segmentation with Multispectral MRI. In: Proc. of ISBI 2010, pp. 648–651 (2010)
13. Liang, J., Bovik, A.: Smoothing Low-SNR Molecular Images via Anisotropic Median-Diffusion. IEEE Trans. on Medical Imaging 21(4), 377–384 (2002)
14. Carrol, C.L., Somer, F.G., McNeal, J.E., Stammey, T.A.: The abnormal prostate: MR Imaging at 1.5-T with histopathologic correlation. Radiology 163, 521–525 (1987)
15. Fisher, R.A.: Statistical Methods for Research Workers. Oliver and Boyd (1954)

# Automatic MRI Atlas-Based External Beam Radiation Therapy Treatment Planning for Prostate Cancer

Jason Dowling[1], Jonathan Lambert[2,3], Joel Parker[2], Peter B. Greer[2,3], Jurgen Fripp[1], James Denham[2,3], Sébastien Ourselin[4], and Olivier Salvado[1]

[1] Australian e-Health Research Centre, CSIRO ICT Centre, Australia
Jason.Dowling@csiro.au
[2] Calvary Mater Newcastle Hospital, Australia
[3] University of Newcastle, Australia
[4] Centre for Medical Image Computing, University College London, UK

**Abstract.** Prostate radiation therapy dose planning currently requires computed tomography (CT) scans as they contain electron density information needed for patient dose calculations. However magnetic resonance imaging (MRI) images have significantly superior soft-tissue contrast for segmenting organs of interest and determining the target volume for treatment. This paper describes work on the development of an alternative treatment workflow enabling both organ delineation and dose planning to be performed using MRI alone. This is achieved by atlas based segmentation and the generation of pseudo-CT scans from MRI. Planning and dosimetry results for three prostate cancer patients from Calvary Mater Newcastle Hospital (Australia) are presented supporting the feasibility of this workflow. Good DSC scores were found for the atlas based segmentation of the prostate (mean 0.84) and bones (mean 0.89). The agreement between MRI/pseudo-CT and CT planning was quantified by dose differences and distance to agreement in corresponding voxels. Dose differences were found to be less than 2%. Chi values indicate that the planning CT and pseudo-CT dose distributions are equivalent.

## 1 Introduction

In Australia, prostate cancer is the most commonly diagnosed cancer behind skin cancer, and is the second highest cause of cancer-related deaths behind lung cancer [1-2]. For Australian men in 2005 prostate cancer was the most prevalent cancer accounting for over 29% of all cancer diagnoses [2]. External beam radiation therapy (EBRT) is a major clinical treatment for prostate cancer. EBRT uses high energy x-ray beams combined from multiple directions to deposit energy (dose) within the patient tumour region (the prostate) to destroy the cancer cells.

The success of image guided radiotherapy depends on the accurate localisation of organs of interest. During prostate cancer radiotherapy treatment there is a need to minimize the dose received by the bladder and rectum (to reduce post-treatment complications). Recent advances in prostate radiotherapy have led to improvements in the amount of dose delivered to target organs, while reducing the amount to organs at risk. However side effects can still include inflammation of the anus, rectal bleeding

A. Madabhushi et al. (Eds.): Prostate Cancer Imaging 2010, LNCS 6367, pp. 25–33, 2010.

and haematuria [3]. MRI has a number of advantages over computed tomography (CT) for treatment planning, including improved soft tissue contrast and better definition of tumour margins [4]. Prostate borders delineated on MRI scans by radiation oncologists have been shown to have lower inter-observer variability and are smaller than on CT [5-7]. Therefore by using MRI extra margins added to account for delineation uncertainties are reduced and less normal tissues irradiated, reducing treatment toxicity.

The main reason why MRI scans are not used for treatment planning is that they are acquired by a completely different physical process related to the magnetic properties of tissues within the body. Tissues with slightly different magnetic properties due for example to the water content will give different MRI image values. Due to the different process MRI scans can not be calibrated to electron density. Radiotherapy dose calculations can therefore not currently be performed on MRI scans. Therefore, if used at all, an MRI scan must be manually aligned to a CT scan to transfer the prostate contour delineated on the MRI scan and dose calculation performed using the CT scan.

The work in this paper aims to develop the first feasible implementation of MRI-based prostate radiation therapy planning. Translating to an MRI based workflow (shown in Fig. 1) involves a number of significant research issues to be addressed, including (i) the development of software for data transfer between the clinical treatment planning system and research software platforms; (ii) methods to automatically segment organs of interest from MRI; and (iii) tools to automatically assign electron density information to MR scans for radiotherapy dose calculations for treatment planning.

## 2   Method

### 2.1   Images

Ethics approval for the study protocol was obtained from the local area health ethics committee and informed consent obtained from all patients. Thirty nine patients had three prostate pure gold fiducial markers of diameter 1.0 mm and length 3.0 mm inserted trans-rectally by a urologist one to two weeks prior to the acquisition of the planning images. Note that results from only three patients are reported in this paper. Both CT and MRI images were acquired, with MRI scans obtained as soon as possible after the CT scans (usually one or two days after). CT scans were acquired either on a GE LightSpeedRT large bore scanner with 2.0 mm slices or a Toshiba Acquilion with 2.5 mm slices. A full bladder and empty rectum were specified. All patients followed a bowel preparation protocol consisting of a high fibre diet. Patients were positioned supine on a rigid couch-top with knee cushions and ankle immobilisation stocks. Three MRI scan sequences were acquired with a GE Medical Systems Signa Excite 1.5 T scanner and pelvic body coil: a $T_2$ wholepelvis MRI (WPMRI) scan, a $T_2$ scan with a smaller FOV for prostate delineation, and a $T_2^*$ scan to image the implanted gold markers. Patients were positioned as closely as possible to the CT scanning position with a 7 mm thick plastic slab placed on the underside of the pelvic coil. For each patient the bone, rectum, bladder and prostate on the CT scan and the WPMRI scan were manually contoured.

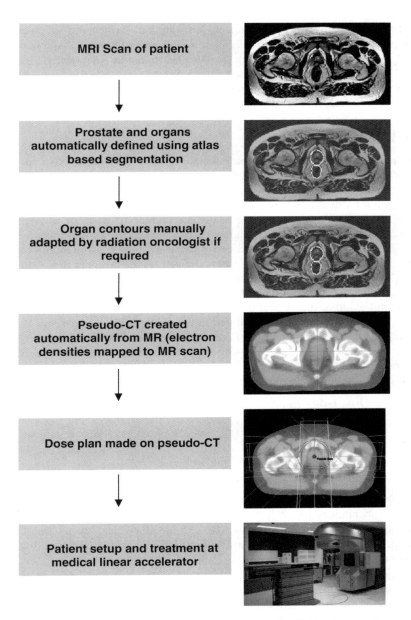

**Fig. 1.** Flow diagram of MRI-based workflow for prostate radiation therapy planning

## 2.2 Treatment Planning System Interface

To perform image analysis tasks, such as automatic segmentation, a method to transfer the image scans, manually defined contours and treatment planning data between commercial treatment planning systems (TPS) and external development software needs to be used. For this project custom software was written and validated for information transfer from the Varian Eclipse and Phillips Pinnacle systems treatment planning at the Mater Hospital (using the DICOM Radiation Therapy extensions (DICOM-RT) and the Radiation Oncology Therapy Group (RTOG) file formats) [8]. To transfer automatic organ segmentations and pseudo-CT images back into these systems for dose validation a modified version of the code written in [9] was used.

## 2.3  MR Atlas Generation

There are few papers on prostate segmentation from MRI (most have focused on ultrasound and CT), however recent papers by Martin et al. [10] and Klein et al. [11] have proposed the use of an automatic prostate segmentation method based on non-rigid registration of a set of pre-labeled MR atlas images. Atlas based segmentation usually involves an atlas image (generally an average of a set of images) with a matching set of organ labels. To segment a new image, the atlas is registered to the the subject's image to obtain a good correspondence between structurally equivalent regions in the two images, and then labels defined on the atlas are propagated to the image [12]. In this paper an atlas-based approach is applied which involves the automatic segmentation of the organs from MR images of the pelvis by generating an average image atlas incorporating non-rigid registration with probabilistic atlases (PAs). The atlas methodology presented in this paper is similar to Klein et al. [11]: the main difference is that instead of identifying a selection of atlas scans which are most similar to the target scan and using only their associated deformed label images, in this paper a single prostate atlas is used.

Before registration, each MR image was pre-processed with:

1. Bias field correction [13];
2. Interleaving correction [14];
3. Anisotropy correction (slice width in each volume resampled from 3 mm to 1.5 mm);
4. Smoothing using anisotropic diffusion;
5. Zero mean and unit variance normalization.

A probabilistic atlas (PA) for each organ of interest was generated by propagating the manual segmentations for each training case using the obtained affine transform and deformation field computed from the MR into the atlas space as per Rohlfing [15]. An arbitrary but representative case in our database was chosen as the initial atlas defining the atlas space alignment

The first iteration involved the registration of every other case to the selected atlas case using rigid followed by affine transformation. Subsequent iterations involved all subjects being registered to the average image using rigid, affine transformation (estimated from correspondences between very similar areas in both images using a block matching approach described in [16]) and non-rigid registration (diffeomorphic demons algorithm [17,18]). At the end of each iteration a new average atlas is generated and used in the subsequent iteration. In the present study, five iterations were performed.

The same method was also used to generate a probabilistic atlas of the prostate from the small field of view T2w images. This atlas was used for prostate segmentation.

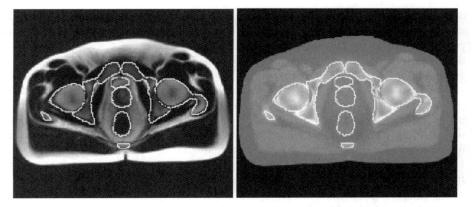

**Fig 2.** Axial view of the whole pelvis MRI atlas (left) and the matching pseudo-CT (right). Organ segmentations have been overlaid (these were thresholded at 50%)

## 2.4 Atlas Generation (CT)

To automatically assign electron density values to a new MR image, we generate a corresponding CT atlas (an axial slice from the whole pelvis MRI atlas and matching pseudo-CT atlas are shown in figure 2). This is achieved by:

1. Multimodal registration of the CT-MR scans for each patient contributing to the atlas. The Insight Toolkit (www.itk.org) implementation was used for rigid and affine registration.
2. Applying the transform matrices and deformation fields from the MR atlas generation described in section 2.3 above to the result of each CT-MR.
3. Generating a median volume from the volumes resulting from step 2.

With regards to step 1, multimodal non-rigid registration was attempted using the Insight Toolkit (www.itk.org) implementation of the free-form deformation algorithm [19]. However this registration method was found to result in unacceptable deformation of bone in the moving image.

The background of the CT atlas was masked to -1000 HU (Air). In addition, a post-generation adjustment of HU units for bone was required as the values for bone were found to be approximately 70HU too low (soft tissue HU values were correct).To correct this random values (Gaussian, mean 70, sd 17.5) were generated and added to voxels in the atlas volume with intensity > 100.

To generate pseudo-CT values for a new patient, the MRI atlas is registered to the patient's MRI. Then the same transformation and deformations are then applied to the CT atlas to create a pseudo-CT corresponding to the patient MR scan anatomy. This pseudo-CT is then used for dose planning and digitally reconstructed radiograph (DRR) generation.

## 2.5 Validation

A leave one out approach was used. Rigid, affine and non-rigid registration were used to map the atlas onto each subject's MR scan and the affine transform and deformation fields were then used to map the organs of interest (prostate, bladder, rectum and bones) onto each scan. These organ PAs were then thresholded (50%) to provide a general segmentation for each individual subject. The automatic segmentations were compared against manual segmentations using the Dice Similarity Coefficient (DSC = 2 ( A ∩ B / (A union B) ) [20].

The spatial accuracy of the MRI scanner was assessed with a spatial uniformity phantom (Fluke Biomedical #76-907, Everett, WA, USA). The phantom was imaged using both the T2 and T2* MRI scan sequences. Measurements on the CT and MRI images of the phantom were made in the horizontal direction to the edges of the phantom and from the centre of the phantom to the corners.

The pseudo-CT images were imported into the corresponding patient in the treatment planning system. The existing treatment plans for each patient were then copied and attached to the pseudo-CT images. While each plan reported 2 Gy at the ICRU point due to the plan prescription, the change in monitor units (MU) was used to compare the dose change for the plans using pseudo-CT images relative to the gold standard plan (which uses the original CT images). If a plan had more than one phase of treatment, each phase was considered separately.

## 3    Results

Dice Similarity Coefficient (DSC) scores between automatic and manual segmentations are summarised in Table 1. The results for prostate segmentation (shown for example Fig. 3) were found to be superior from the small field of view atlas. The bladder and rectum showed greater variability between atlas subjects with corresponding lower scores.

**Fig 3.** Coronal, Sagittal and Axial views of small field of view MR scan from patient H028. The automatic prostate segmentation has been overlaid.

**Table 1.** DSC scores between manual and automatic segmentations for each pelvic organ For the three patients. SFOV = MRI small field of view, WPFOV = MRI whole pelvis field of view

| Patient | Prostate (SFOV) | Prostate (WPFOV) | Rectum | Bladder | Bone |
|---------|-----------------|------------------|--------|---------|------|
| E027 | 0.85 | 0.74 | 0.67 | 0.43 | 0.88 |
| H028 | 0.83 | 0.78 | 0.63 | 0.75 | 0.89 |
| R031 | 0.84 | 0.84 | 0.65 | 0.73 | 0.89 |
| **Mean (sd)** | 0.84 (0.01) | 0.79 (0.05) | 0.65 (0.02) | 0.64 (0.18) | 0.89 (0.01) |

Six plans in total were calculated from the three patients (one patient had two phases of treatment, and one had three phases). Based on the doses calculated using the reported monitor units, the doses from the three patients ranged from 1.94 Gy to 1.99 Gy (2.8% to 0.6% lower than the intended 2 Gy). Digitally reconstructed radiographs from one patient's pseudo-CT are shown in Fig. 4. The automatic contours and dose plan for the same patient are shown in Fig. 5.

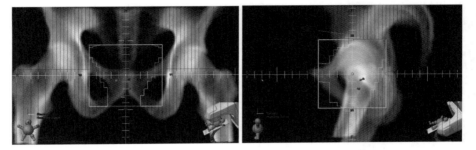

**Fig 4.** Anterior-posterior (AP) (left) and lateral digitally reconstructed radiographs generated from the MRI pseudo-CT volume for patient H028.

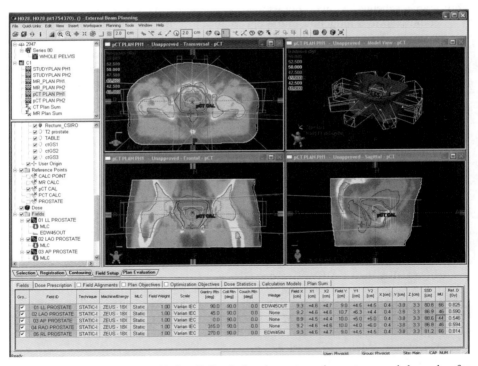

**Fig 5.** Screenshot from TPS (Varian Eclipse) showing automatic contours and dose plan for patient H028. The dose plan shows the beam arrangement (two lateral, one anterior and two oblique fields) and the dose deposited due to these beams.

The pseudo-CT and original CT plans of the three patients were quantified using the Chi comparison value [21] applied to the 3D dose distributions: any value over 80% of the maximum dose and all Chi values fall in the region of -1 to 1 indicating that the dose distributions are equivalent.

Small spatial distortions were found in the MRI scanner but these were at most 2-3 mm at more than 20 cm from the centre of the scanner. These small distortions are not sufficient to introduce significant errors in dose calculations for pelvic radiotherapy. Small distortions will be present in DRRs however these will be very small at the centre of the scan where the prostate fiducial markers are located.

## 4 Discussion and Conclusion

The feasibility of MRI based radiation therapy for prostate cancer has been established. The difference between dose from the planning CT and the MRI based pseudo-CT was found to be less than 2%. Chi value analysis indicates that the dose distributions for all three patients were equivalent. Further optimization of the method and validation of the accuracy of MRI-based dose plans with a larger patient data set is ongoing.

The automatic segmentation of the prostate from axial MR images using a probability atlas scheme had good correspondence with the manual segmentation results. This could lead to a reduction in the uncertainties in prostate segmentation for prostate treatment. Better knowledge of the location of the prostate border will result in less normal tissues receiving unnecessary and harmful high doses of radiation with subsequently fewer and less severe side-effects of treatment. The automatic segmentation results for the rectum and bladder may provide useful initial constraints for further segmentation methods (for example, by masking and then using active contours within the masked region).

The work is ongoing and further validation of the pseudo-CT and automatically defined contours against standard CT based treatment planning are occurring.

**Acknowledgments.** This work was partially funded by the Cancer Council NSW, Project Grant RG 07-06.

## References

1. Australian Institute of Health and Welfare (AIHW): Australian Cancer Incidence and Mortality (ACIM) Books. AIHW, Canberra (2007)
2. Australian Institute of Health and Welfare (AIHW) and Australasian Association of Cancer Registries (AACR): Cancer in Australia: an overview, 2008. AIHW, Canberra (2008)
3. Swallow, T., Kirby, R.: Cancer of the prostate gland. Surgery 26(5), 213–217 (2008)
4. Prabhakar, R., et al.: Feasibility of using MRI alone for 3D radiation treatment planning in brain tumors. Jpn. J. Clin. Oncol. 37(6), 405–411 (2007)
5. Roach, M., et al.: Prostate volumes defined by Magnetic Resonance Imaging and computerized tomographic scans for three-dimensional conformal radiotherapy. Int. J. Radiat. Oncol. Biol. Phys. 35(5), 1011–1018 (1996)

6. Debois, M., et al.: The contribution of magnetic resonance imaging to the three-dimensional treatment planning of localized prostate cancer. Int. J. Radiat. Oncol. Biol. Phys. 45(4), 857–865 (1999)
7. Rasch, C., et al.: Definition of the prostate in CT and MRI: a multi-observer study. Int. J. Radiat. Oncol. Biol. Phys. 43(1), 57–66 (1999)
8. Dowling, J., et al.: Importing Contours from DICOM-RT structure sets. Insight Journal (July-December 2009)
9. Gorthi, S., et al.: Exporting Contours to DICOM-RT Structure Set. Insight Journal (January-June 2009)
10. Martin, S., et al.: Atlas-based prostate segmentation using an hybrid registration. Int. J. CARS 3, 485–492 (2008)
11. Klein, S., et al.: Automatic segmentation of the prostate in 3D MR images by atlas matching using localized mutual information. Med. Phys. 35(4), 1407–1417 (2008)
12. Crum, W.R., et al.: Non-rigid image registration: theory and practice. Br. J. Radiol. 77(spec No. 2), S140–S153 (2004)
13. Salvado, O., et al.: Method to correct intensity inhomogeneity in MR images for atherosclerosis characterization. IEEE Trans. Med. Imaging 25(5), 539–552 (2006)
14. Dowling, J., et al.: Nonrigid correction of interleaving artefacts in pelvic MRI. In: Pluim, J.P.W., Dawant, B.M. (eds.) SPIE MI, p. 72592P (2009)
15. Rohlfing, T., et al.: Evaluation of atlas selection strategies for atlas-based image segmentation with application to confocal microscopy images of bee brains. Neuroimage 21(4), 1428–1442 (2004)
16. Ourselin, S., et al.: Reconstructing a 3D Structure from Serial Histological Sections. Image and Vision Computing 19(1-2), 25–31 (2001)
17. Vercauteren, T., et al.: Non-parametric diffeomorphic image registration with the demons algorithm. In: Ayache, N., Ourselin, S., Maeder, A. (eds.) MICCAI 2007, Part II. LNCS, vol. 4792, pp. 319–326. Springer, Heidelberg (2007)
18. Vercauteren, T., et al.: Diffeomorphic demons using ITK's finite difference solver hierarchy. The Insight Journal (2007)
19. Rueckert, D., Sonoda, L.I., Hayes, C., Hill, D.L., Leach, M.O., Hawkes, D.J.: Nonrigid registration using free-form deformations: application to breast MR images. IEEE Transactions on Medical Imaging 18, 712–721 (1999)
20. Dice, L.R.: Measures of the Amount of Ecologic Association Between Species. Ecology 26(3), 297–302 (1945)
21. Bakai, A., et al.: A revision of the $\gamma$-evaluation concept for the comparison of dose distributions. Phys. Med. Biol. 48, 3543–3553 (2003)

# An Efficient Inverse-Consistent Diffeomorphic Image Registration Method for Prostate Adaptive Radiotherapy

Xiao Han, Lyndon S. Hibbard, and Virgil Willcut

Elekta CMS Software, 13723 Riverport Drive, St. Louis, MO 63043, USA

**Abstract.** Deformable image registration is a key enabling technology for adaptive radiation therapy (ART) as it can facilitate structure segmentation as well as dose tracking and accumulation. In this work, we develop an efficient inverse-consistent diffeomorphic registration method applying the log-Euclidean formulation of diffeomorphisms. Unlike existing log-Euclidean deformable registration approaches, the proposed method deforms two images towards each other in a completely symmetric fashion during the registration optimization, which leads to higher efficiency and better accuracy in recovering large deformations. The method is applied for the automatic segmentation of daily CT images in prostate ART. To address difficulties caused by large bladder and rectum content change, we propose further improvements and combine deformable registration with model-based image segmentation. Validation results on real clinical data showed that the proposed method gives highly accurate segmentation of interested structures.

## 1 Introduction

Adaptive radiation therapy (ART) has emerged as an important treatment technology for cancer patients, with the goal of delivering high precision treatment by adapting to daily changes in patient anatomy. Deformable image registration is an indispensable method for the successful implementation of ART, as it can greatly facilitate structure auto-segmentation and dose tracking and accumulation. For example, with the estimated image correspondence from deformable image registration, contours on the planning image can be mapped to the daily treatment images to get their automatic segmentation, a process often referred to as *automatic re-contouring*. The anatomical correspondence can also be used to map the delivered treatment dose to a reference frame, allowing cumulative dose to be computed and compared to the original plan. For ART applications, a desirable property of a useful non-linear registration method is that the registration result should be invariant with respect to the order of the input images, which is known as the inverse-consistency criterion. Inverse consistency reduces registration bias and allows contour or dose information to be consistently mapped between different image frames.

A. Madabhushi et al. (Eds.): Prostate Cancer Imaging 2010, LNCS 6367, pp. 34–41, 2010.

Inverse-consistent deformable image registration has been the subject of extensive study in the literature (cf. [1,2,3,4,5,6] and references therein). Existing methods typically have high computational cost due to the need for explicitly computing both the forward and the backward transformations and sometimes also their inverses. The recent introduction of the stationary log-Euclidean representation of diffeomorphisms [7] allows the use of a single vector field to model both the forward and inverse transformations, which can significantly simplify the formulation of inverse-consistent deformable registration methods. The three existing methods [4,8,9] in this framework all employ a symmetric cost function design that involves two separate image similarity terms, one for the forward transformation and one for its inverse. In this work, we simplify the formulation in order to get a more efficient algorithm. Most importantly, with our formulation, the two images to be registered are deformed towards each other in a completely symmetric fashion during the optimization process, which improves both the efficiency and accuracy for recovering large deformations. We note that similar symmetric deformation ideas have been proposed by others in the literature [5,3], but the overall formulation is different and computationally more expensive.

In this work, we further adapt the proposed inverse-consistent deformable registration method for the auto-recontouring of treatment CT images for prostate ART. To address difficulty caused by the overlapping of bladder with nearby structures with similar intensity, we propose to combine image registration with model-based bladder segmentation. Special pre-processing to improve registration accuracy in the presence of large rectum content change is also developed. In the following, we first present our new inverse-consistent deformable registration framework and then describe the complete algorithm for prostate CT image auto-recontouring.

## 2   Inverse-Consistent Diffeomorphic Registration

Given two images $I, J : \mathcal{R}^3 \mapsto \mathcal{R}$, the goal of image registration is to find a well-behaved spatial transformation $T(I, J)$ that aligns points in one image to their corresponding points in the other. Mathematically, image registration can be formulated as an optimization problem:

$$T_{\text{opt}} = \text{argmax}_{T \in \Omega_T} \text{Sim}(I, J, T), \tag{1}$$

where $T_{\text{opt}}$ denotes the optimal transformation, $\text{Sim}(\cdot)$ is a selected similarity metric and $\Omega_T$ denotes the space of all feasible transformations. In this work, we require the image transformation $T$ to be a diffeomorphic mapping, i.e., $T$ is globally one-to-one, smooth, and has a smooth inverse.

The Large Deformation Diffeomorphic Metric Mapping (LDDMM) has been considered as the standard paradigm for diffeomorphic registration in Computational Anatomy (cf. [10,8]), where diffeomorphic transformations are represented through geodesic paths of time-varying vector fields. A major disadvantage of this framework is its high computational cost. Recently, a log-Euclidean framework was proposed by Arsigny et al. [7] that represents a diffeomorphic mapping as the group exponential map of a stationary vector or velocity field, i.e.,

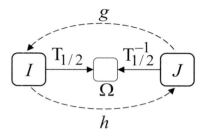

**Fig. 1.** Symmetric Registration Framework

$T = \exp(\mathbf{V})$. In addition, the exponential map can be computed efficiently using a "scaling-and-squaring" method [7]. Although the stationary formulation has fewer degrees of freedom than the original LDDMM model, it has been shown to be versatile enough and led to the the development of new diffeomorphic registration algorithms with better computation efficiency [4,8,9].

We adopt the same stationary velocity field parametrization to develop a new inverse-consistent diffeomorphic image registration method. Unlike the previous work [4,8,9], we propose to deform both images simultaneously and in a completely symmetric fashion. As illustrated in Fig. 1, we aim to compute a pair of half-way transformations and enforce them to be exact inverse of each other. Using the log-Euclidean framework, we can represent both half-way transformations using a single velocity field $\mathbf{V}$: $\mathrm{T}_{1/2} = \exp(\mathbf{V})$, and $\mathrm{T}_{1/2}^{-1} = \exp(-\mathbf{V})$, as it is known that $\exp(-\mathbf{V})$ and $\exp(\mathbf{V})$ are exact inverse transformations of each other. After registration, the complete forward transformation can be computed as $h = \exp(\mathbf{V}) \circ \exp(-\mathbf{V})^{-1} = \exp(2\mathbf{V})$ and the backward one by $g = \exp(-2\mathbf{V})$, where "$\circ$" denotes transformation composition.

We build this symmetric transformation model into an intensity-based deformable registration method. In this work, the sum-of-squared-differences (SSD) is used as the image similarity metric since it performs well for CT images; but other metrics can also be applied and the derivation is similar. With the above model, Eq. (1) can be reformulated as

$$\mathbf{V}_{\mathrm{opt}} = \mathrm{argmin}_{\mathbf{V}} \|I \circ \exp(-\mathbf{V}) - J \circ \exp(\mathbf{V})\|^2 + \lambda \|\mathcal{L}\mathbf{V}\|^2, \qquad (2)$$

where $\|\cdot\|$ denotes the $L^2$-norm and $\mathcal{L}$ denotes a proper linear differential operator that penalizes irregularity of the vector field $\mathbf{V}$.

We compute the optimal solution of Eq. (2) using an iterative algorithm following the "pair-and-smooth" strategy proposed in [11]: at each iteration we first update the vector field $\mathbf{V}$ to optimize the similarity measure and then smooth the new vector field estimation. The weighting factor $\lambda$ is not explicitly used but is reflected in the selection of the kernel width of the smoothing filter applied for the vector field regularization.

More specifically, given the current estimation of the vector field $\mathbf{V}^n$ where $n$ denotes the iteration number, we first seek an update field $\mathbf{u}^n$ that minimizes

$$\|I \circ \exp(-\mathbf{V}^n) \circ \exp(-\mathbf{u}^n), J \circ \exp(\mathbf{V}^n) \circ \exp(\mathbf{u}^n)\|^2. \qquad (3)$$

To simplify, let $I^n = I \circ \exp(-\mathbf{V}^n)$ denote the transformed image $I$ by applying the backward half-transformation at iteration $n$ and $J^n = J \circ \exp(\mathbf{V}^n)$ the transformed image $J$ by the forward half-transformation. Then the optimal $\mathbf{u}^n$ should minimize

$$\mathrm{SSD}(I^n, J^n, \mathbf{u}^n) = \|I^n \circ \exp(-\mathbf{u}^n) - J^n \circ \exp(\mathbf{u}^n)\|^2. \tag{4}$$

Considering only small updates at each iteration, we have $\exp(\mathbf{u}^n) \approx \mathbf{Id} + \mathbf{u}^n$, where $\mathbf{Id}$ denotes the identity transformation. Substituting it into Eq. (4) and applying the Gauss-Newton rule, the optimal update field can be found as

$$\mathbf{u}^n(\mathbf{x}) = -H^{-1}(\mathbf{x})(I^n(\mathbf{x}) - J^n(\mathbf{x}))(\nabla I^n(\mathbf{x}) + \nabla J^n(\mathbf{x})), \tag{5}$$

where $H(\mathbf{x})$ is the $3 \times 3$ Hessian matrix given by

$$H = (\nabla I^n + \nabla J^n)(\nabla I^n + \nabla J^n)^T + (I^n - J^n)(\Delta I^n - \Delta J^n). \tag{6}$$

Given $\mathbf{u}^n$, we can compute two intermediate updates for $\mathbf{V}^n$, corresponding to the forward and the backward half-transformations respectively:

$$\mathbf{V}_f^{n+1} = \log(\exp(\mathbf{V}^n) \circ \exp(\mathbf{u}^n)), \tag{7}$$

$$\mathbf{V}_b^{n+1} = -\log(\exp(-\mathbf{V}^n) \circ \exp(-\mathbf{u}^n)). \tag{8}$$

The logarithm map in the above equations can be computed efficiently using the Baker-Campbell-Hausdorff (BCH) formula proposed in [12].

In general, $\mathbf{V}_b^{n+1} \neq \mathbf{V}_f^{n+1}$; hence the transformations for the two images are no longer symmetric if either Eq. (7) or Eq. (8) is used. To maintain complete symmetry and ensure inverse-consistency, we compute the final updated velocity field $\mathbf{V}^{n+1}$ as

$$\mathbf{V}^{n+1} = \frac{1}{2} \log(\exp(\mathbf{V}_f^{n+1}) \circ \exp(\mathbf{V}_b^{n+1})). \tag{9}$$

This is equivalent to first computing the full transformation by composing the forward and backward half-transforms and then split it into two equal halves.

After $\mathbf{V}^{n+1}$ is computed, we regularize it using a spatial Gaussian filter, and then start the next iteration. The iterative update is repeated until a user-specified number of steps or until the SSD metric stops decreasing. The overall method is summarized in Algorithm 1 below. It can be easily checked that the algorithm is fully inverse consistent. In fact, the algorithm guarantees that $\mathbf{V}_{I \rightarrow J}^n = -\mathbf{V}_{J \rightarrow I}^n$ at every iteration of the algorithm, where $V_{I \rightarrow J}^n$ denotes the velocity field at iteration $n$ with input images $I$ and $J$ and $V_{J \rightarrow I}^n$ denotes the velocity field at the same iteration but with the order of the two images switched. To improve computational efficiency, the traditional multi-resolution scheme can be applied, which runs Algorithm 1 in a coarse-to-fine fashion using a pyramid representation of both images.

Fig. 2 shows one example that compares the proposed method with the symmetric log-domain Demons registration method of [9]. The results of both methods were computed under similar parameter settings. It is clear that our method

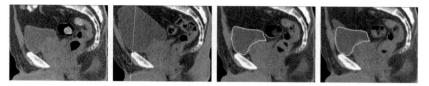

**Fig. 2.** Comparison of the proposed method with that of [9]. The first two are the original images. The third one is the second image aligned to the first using the proposed method, and the last is the result using [9]. The contours on the last two images correspond to the bladder outline of the first image.

aligns the bladder much better due to the proposed symmetric, simultaneous deformation model. In addition, it typically requires fewer iterations before convergence, thus offering better efficiency.

**Algorithm 1. (Symmetric Inverse-Consistent Diffeomorphic Registration):**

0. Given two images $I, J$, and an initial estimate $\mathbf{V}^0$, set $n = 0$.
1. Compute forward transformation $\exp(\mathbf{V}^n)$, and $J^n = J \circ \exp(\mathbf{V}^n)$;
2. Compute backward transformation $\exp(-\mathbf{V}^n)$, and $I^n = I \circ \exp(-\mathbf{V}^n)$;
3. Compute update $\mathbf{u}^n$ using Eq. (5);
4. Compute $\mathbf{V}^{(n+1)}$ using Eqs. (7), (8), and (9);
5. Regularize $\mathbf{V}^{(n+1)}$ with a spatial Gaussian filter;
6. If converged, stop; otherwise, set $n = n + 1$, goto Step 1.

# 3   Prostate Image Auto-Recontouring

A main application of the proposed deformable registration method that we consider in this work is the automated re-contouring of treatment CT images in prostate ART. As mentioned earlier, this is achieved through deformable registration of each treatment image to the already segmented planning CT image of the same patient. In this application, a major complication factor that often limits the registration accuracy is large bladder and rectum content change that can happen between planning and treatment time. As observed by others [13], the presence of rectal gas can cause significant correspondence errors as no correspondence exists for pockets of gas across different days. Although large bladder deformation by itself is not a problem for the proposed method, difficulty arises when an enlarged bladder in one image is overlapped with another structure with similar image intensities in the second image, such as the bowel. Similar intensity of difference structures leads to local optimum of the image similarity metric, which cannot be easily resolved using image registration method alone.

We address these difficulties through proper image preprocessing and bladder pre-segmentation. To account for rectum content change, we apply a simple image thresholding to detect gas pockets in each input image and then modify the image intensity at detected voxels to the average intensity of solid rectum tissues. To account for large bladder shape changes, we have developed a deformable surface model method for bladder segmentation in the treatment image $J$:

$$\mathbf{d}_{\text{opt}} = \text{argmin}_{\mathbf{d}} \int \int \exp(-\|\nabla J(\mathbf{x}_0 + \mathbf{d}(r, s))\|^2) dr ds + \int \int \|\nabla \mathbf{d}(r, s)\|^2 dr ds. \tag{10}$$

In the above equation, $\mathbf{x}_0$ denotes the center of the surface model and $\mathbf{d}(r, s)$ indicates the radius vector at each surface vertex (indexed by $(r, s)$). As indicated in the above equation, each surface vertex is only allowed to deform along the radial direction, which helps maintain a star-like shape of the deforming surface and prevents leaking. In addition, the smoothness constraint as indicated in the second term of Eq. (10) also keeps the surface and its deformation to be smooth. We initialize the model as a small sphere interior to the bladder based on the mapped planning bladder surface after an initial linear registration. The model is then iteratively updated according to a gradient-descent optimization of Eq. (10). The surface centroid $\mathbf{x}_0$ is also updated after each iteration. At convergence, the final bladder surface location of each vertex is computed using $\mathbf{x}(r, s) = \mathbf{x}_0 + \mathbf{d}(r, s)$. An example result is shown in Fig. 3 below.

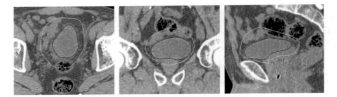

**Fig. 3.** Cross-sectional views of a model-based bladder segmentation result. The thin yellow curves correspond to the mapped planning bladder surface after linear registration, and the red curves are the deformable model bladder segmentation result.

After the bladder is segmented, the bladder surfaces in both planning and treatment images are converted to two signed distance functions and used as an extra channel to the SSD metric. The symmetric, inverse-consistent registration method described in the previous section can be similarly applied.

## 4   Results

To evaluate the performance of the proposed method, we applied it to a set of 24 clinical CT images from 6 patients (4 images for each patient). The images have a voxel size about $0.85 \times 0.85 \times 1.5\text{mm}^3$. Four structures were manually delineated by experts for each image: the bladder, the rectum, the prostate, and the seminal vesicles (SV). The proposed image registration and auto-recontouring method was applied to map structure contours from the first image of each patient to the remaining three images.

Fig. 4 illustrates the segmentation result for one patient. The top row shows the planning image with given manual contours, and the bottom row shows

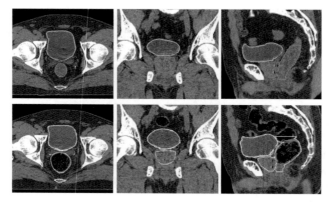

**Fig. 4.** Illustration of an auto-recontouring result (see text for details)

the treatment image with auto-segmentation results (the color curves) using the proposed method. This is a challenging case due to large rectum shape and content change between the planning and treatment images. The method gives very accurate results for all four structures, which agree very well with the given manual segmentation (the white curves) on the treatment image.

For quantitative evaluation, we computed the widely used Dice similarity coefficient (DSC) between the the auto- and manual- segmentation results. The overall statistics of the DSC values are summarized in the box and whisker plots of Fig. 5, where the left plot summarizes the results by directly applying the deformable registration method and the right summarizes the results of the complete algorithm with rectum and bladder processing. It can be seen that the proposed deformable registration method itself already performs very well except for a few outliers corresponding to cases with large bladder and rectum content change. The rectal gas detection and bladder model addressed this difficulty and produces significantly better accuracy. The results also compare favorably with other reported prostate auto-recontouring methods in the literature [13].

We have implemented the proposed deformable registration method on GPU using the NVIDIA CUDA programming model, and it usually takes less than one minute to process one pair of images on a desktop computer with an Intel Xeon Quad-core 2.66GHz CPU and a NVIDIA GTX 280 graphics card.

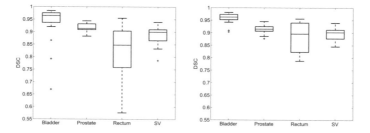

**Fig. 5.** Box plots of DSC results for 4 structures (see text for details.)

# 5   Conclusion

In this work, we developed a fully symmetric, inverse-consistent diffeomorphic registration method and adapted it to the automatic segmentation of daily CT images for prostate adaptive radiotherapy. The proposed registration method deforms both images towards each other in a completely symmetric fashion, which is shown to be more effective in recovering large deformations. Combined with rectal gas detection and model-based bladder segmentation, the overall method gives very high accuracy for the segmentation of real CT images. Future work includes validation on a larger set of data, and evaluating the registration accuracy for dose accumulation applications. It is also desirable to extend the proposed method for the segmentation of CBCT images.

# References

1. Christensen, G.E., Johnson, H.J.: Consistent image registration. IEEE Transactions on Medical Imaging 20(7), 568–582 (2001)
2. Joshi, S., David, B., Jomier, M., Gerig, G.: Unbiased diffeomorphic atlas construction for computational anatomy. NeuroImage 23, S151–S160 (2004)
3. Beg, M., Khan, A.: Symmetric data attachment terms for large deformation image registration. IEEE Trans. Med. Imag. 26, 1179–1189 (2007)
4. Ashburner, J.: A fast diffeomorphic image registration algorithm. NeuroImage 38, 95–113 (2007)
5. Avants, B., Epstein, C., Grossman, M., Gee, J.: Symmetric diffeomorphic image registration with cross-correlation. Med. Imag. Anal. 12, 26–41 (2008)
6. Ye, X., Chen, Y.: A new algorithm for inverse consistent image registration. In: Bebis, G., Boyle, R., Parvin, B., Koracin, D., Kuno, Y., Wang, J., Wang, J.-X., Wang, J., Pajarola, R., Lindstrom, P., Hinkenjann, A., Encarnação, M.L., Silva, C.T., Coming, D. (eds.) ISVC 2009, Part I. LNCS, vol. 5875, pp. 855–864. Springer, Heidelberg (2009)
7. Arsigny, V., Commowick, O., Pennec, X., Ayache, N.: A Log-Euclidean framework for statistics on diffeomorphisms. In: Larsen, R., Nielsen, M., Sporring, J. (eds.) MICCAI 2006. LNCS, vol. 4190, pp. 924–931. Springer, Heidelberg (2006)
8. Hernandez, M., Bossa, M., Olmos, S.: Registration of anatomical images using geodesic paths of diffeomorphisms parameterized with stationary vector fields. In: Proc. of ICCV 2007, Los Alamitos, CA, USA, pp. 1–8 (2007)
9. Vercauteren, T., Pennec, X., Perchant, A., Ayache, N.: Symmetric Log-domain diffeomorphic registration: A Demons-based approach. In: Metaxas, D., Axel, L., Fichtinger, G., Székely, G. (eds.) MICCAI 2008, Part I. LNCS, vol. 5241, pp. 754–761. Springer, Heidelberg (2008)
10. Beg, M., Miller, M., Trouvé, A., Younes, L.: Computing large deformation metric mapping via geodesic flows of diffeomorphisms. Int. J. Comput. Vis. 61, 139–157 (2005)
11. Cachier, P., Ayache, N.: How to trade off between regularization and image similarity in non-rigid registration? In: Niessen, W.J., Viergever, M.A. (eds.) MICCAI 2001. LNCS, vol. 2208, pp. 1285–1286. Springer, Heidelberg (2001)
12. Bossa, M., Hernandez, M., Olmos, S.: Contributions to 3D diffeomorphic atlas estimation. In: Ayache, N., Ourselin, S., Maeder, A. (eds.) MICCAI 2007, Part I. LNCS, vol. 4791, pp. 667–674. Springer, Heidelberg (2007)
13. Foskey, M., Davis, B., Goyal, L., Chang, S., Chaney, E., Strehl, N., Tomei, S., Rosenman, J., Joshi, S.: Large deformation three-dimensional image registration in image-guided radiation therapy. Phys. Med. Biol. 50, 5869–5892 (2005)

# Atlas Based Segmentation and Mapping of Organs at Risk from Planning CT for the Development of Voxel-Wise Predictive Models of Toxicity in Prostate Radiotherapy

Oscar Acosta[1,2], Jason Dowling[4], Guillaume Cazoulat[1,2], Antoine Simon[1,2], Olivier Salvado[4], Renaud de Crevoisier[1,2,3], and Pascal Haigron[1,2]

[1] INSERM, U 642, Rennes, F-35000, France
[2] Université de Rennes 1, LTSI, F-35000, France
{guillaume.cazoulat,antoine.simon,oscar.acosta}@univ-rennes1.fr
pascal.haigron@univ-rennes1.fr
[3] Département de Radiothérapie, Centre Eugène Marquis, Rennes, F-35000, France
r.de-crevoisier@rennes.fnclcc.fr
[4] The Australian e-Health Research Centre, CSIRO ICT Centre, Brisbane, Australia
{Jason.Dowling, Olivier.Salvado}@csiro.au

**Abstract.** The prediction of toxicity is crucial to managing prostate cancer radiotherapy (RT). This prediction is classically organ wise and based on the dose volume histograms (DVH) computed during the planning step, and using for example the mathematical Lyman Normal Tissue Complication Probability (NTCP) model. However, these models lack spatial accuracy, do not take into account deformations and may be inappropiate to explain toxicity events related with the distribution of the delivered dose. Producing voxel wise statistical models of toxicity might help to explain the risks linked to the dose spatial distribution but is challenging due to the difficulties lying on the mapping of organs and dose in a common template. In this paper we investigate the use of atlas based methods to perform the non-rigid mapping and segmentation of the individuals' organs at risk (OAR) from CT scans. To build a labeled atlas, 19 CT scans were selected from a population of patients treated for prostate cancer by radiotherapy. The prostate and the OAR (Rectum, Bladder, Bones) were then manually delineated by an expert and constituted the training data. After a number of affine and non rigid registration iterations, an average image (template) representing the whole population was obtained. The amount of consensus between labels was used to generate probabilistic maps for each organ. We validated the accuracy of the approach by segmenting the organs using the training data in a leave one out scheme. The agreement between the volumes after deformable registration and the manually segmented organs was on average above 60% for the organs at risk. The proposed methodology provides a way to map the organs from a whole population on a single template and sets the stage to perform further voxel wise analysis. With this method new and accurate predictive models of toxicity will be built.

## 1 Introduction

The main challenge in prostate cancer radiotherapy is to deliver the prescribed dose to the clinical target while minimising the dose to the organs at risk (OAR), thus

A. Madabhushi et al. (Eds.): Prostate Cancer Imaging 2010, LNCS 6367, pp. 42–51, 2010.

avoiding subsequent toxicity-related events [1]. The prediction of toxicity is central to improving the reliability of the treatment [2]. Dose-volume histograms (DVH) [3], tying together the dose received by the patient and the irradiated volumes, have been largely used to estimate the risk of complications. These values may also be fitted with the Lyman Normal Tissue Complication Probability (NTCP) to predict toxicity[4,5,6]. In this way, many studies have shown a correlation between dose, volume and rectal toxicity [7,8,9,10,11,12]. For the bladder, these correlations are however very limited [13]. Based on these studies, different recommendations for the rectum and bladder dose-volume values have been defined, but corresponding to a small number of threshold values.

Although the recommandations are precise in terms of DVH, it has been pointed that the DVH and NTCP models may lack specificity for prediction. The likelihood of toxicity related events depends not only on the dose and the volume of the organs included in the radiation field [7,14] but also on individual's specific factors, such as radiosensitivity or personal medical history [15]. In addition, anatomical deformations may occur during treatment and consequently the planned dose does not fit to the actual delivered dose [16], leading to uncertainties in NTCP calculation. Finally, there is a lack of spatial specificty in the models which would grant a voxel-wise link between delivered dose and the surgical outcome and toxicity, to a large extent.

More accurate predictive models that include a large set of explanatory variables and allow an increased spatial specificity have to be developed to test toxicity hypothesis. Cumulative DVH, for instance, being more representative of the actual received dose [17] should lead to more reliable computation. The importance of spatial location has also been pointed out by [18]. More recently published papers already performed voxel wise analysis in two populations to statistically compare toxicity outcomes in the urinary tract [19] and tumor control in the prostate [20]. However the methods used to map the organs to a single template rely on organ delineations and are approximated in terms of spatial location. Thus, the mapping was defined by a parametric representation of the whole image with respect to the organs position in polar coordinates. A more accurate mapping of the organs at risk and in overall of the whole pelvic region at a voxel basis is therefore needed allowing to relate the outcome of the treatment to the delivered dose.

We present in this paper an atlas based method for the non-rigid mapping of the individuals' organs at risk (OAR) to a single template and evaluate its accuracy performing the segmentation of the main organs in their native space. We would like to raise awareness about the increasing necessity of spatial specific predictive models for toxicity and discuss about the problems brought by the mapping of OAR to a single template for further voxel-wise analysis. We developed an atlas-based approach based on the methodology presented by [21], except that ours is based only on the CT used during the planning in the clinical practice. To constitute the training data, 19 individuals' CT scans were manually delineated by an expert (prostate and the OAR). To validate the mapping, the volume overlap was computed based on the manual segmentations of the main organs from the CT scans.

## 2    Method

### 2.1    Patient Data

The training set consisted of nineteen patients treated for prostate cancer, who underwent a planning CT scan and 8 more weekly CT scans. All CT scans were acquired without constrast enhancement. The size of the images in the axial plane was 512*512 pixels with 1 mm resolution 3-mm thick slices. For each patient, the femur, the bladder, the rectum, the prostate and the seminal vesicles (SV) were manually contoured by the same observer.

### 2.2    Atlas Generation

A probabilistic atlas was generated by using the same methodology as presented by Dowling et al. [21] for MRI segmentation who extended the approach proposed by Rohlfing [22]. Probabilistic labels for the prostate, rectum, bladder and bones were generated by propagating the manual segmentations of these organs for each case using the obtained affine transform and deformation field computed from the MR into the atlas space as per Rohlfing [22]. An arbitrary but representative case in our database was chosen as the initial atlas, defining the atlas space alignment. The first iteration involved the registration of every other case to the selected individual case using a robust block matching approach [23], followed by a diffeomorphic Demons non-rigid registration [24] in the subsequent iterations. At the end of each iteration a new average atlas is generated and used in the subsequent iteration. In the present study, five iterations were performed. Fig. 1 shows the obtained atlas and an overlaid of the probabilistic labeling for the prostate and the rectum in the atlas coordinate system.

### 2.3    Segmentation of Organs from the Planning CT

After generation of the probabilistic labels (Prostate, rectum, bladder, femur and seminal vesicles) in the common space, the atlas was used in a segmentation step to constrain the organs of interest. Thus, a scheme based on affine [23], followed by a diffeomorphic

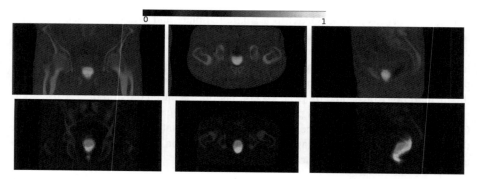

**Fig. 1.** *Top*: Prostate and *Bottom*: Rectum probability maps overlaid on the generated atlas orthogonal slices

Demons non-rigid registration [24] led us to map the atlas onto each individual's CT scan. The obtained affine transform and deformation fields were then used to map the probabilistic labels onto each individual scan. These registered labels were thresholded (at 50%) to provide the hard organ segmentations for each individual scan. The overall process is depicted in Fig. 2. We also tested different levels of thresholding and for the prostate the results are depicted in Fig. 5, but 50% threshold represented a good compromise between all the organs.

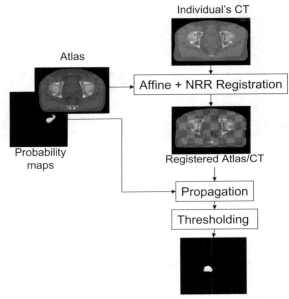

**Fig. 2.** Atlas based segmentation process from the planning CT

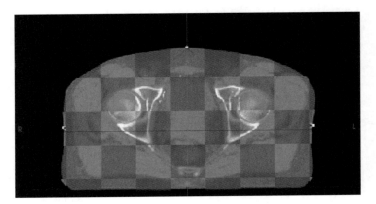

**Fig. 3.** Example of registration between the atlas and a single individual

Figure 3 depicts the overlap between the atlas and a single individual. With the used non rigid registration scheme good coincidence between the two images is obtained, although the soft tissus are not as visible as they can be in an MRI. Notably the bladder and rectum fits better with the template than the prostate, because the contrast in those organs is higher.

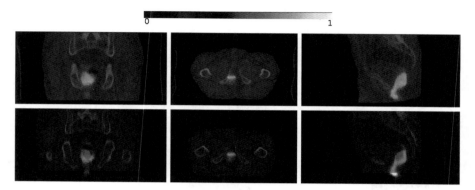

**Fig. 4.** *Top*: Rectum probability map overlaid on the atlas coordinate system. *Bottom*: the rectum probability map is propagated to one individual's CT scan after registration.

## 3   Results

Using affine registration followed by the Demons algorithm for non-rigid registration, the automatic segmentation for each CT scan required approximately 14 minutes on a Dell T5500, with 12 Gb RAM, dual quad core (Quad-Core Intel(R) Xeon(R) X5550 (2.66Ghz/8MB L3 Cache).

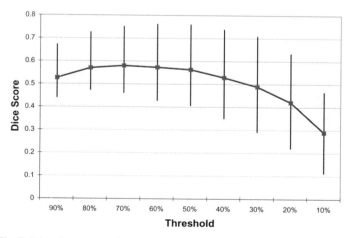

**Fig. 5.** Dice Scores as a function of the prostate probability map threshold

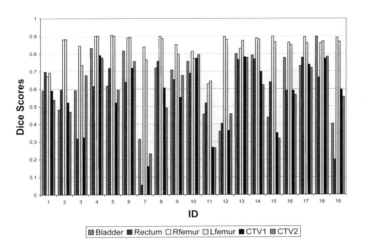

**Fig. 6.** Leave one out validation. Dice Scores for all the labeled organs (CTV2=:prostate, CTV1:prostate and Seminal Vesicles).

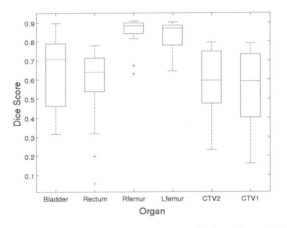

**Fig. 7.** Leave one out validation. Dice Scores distribution for all the labeled organs (CTV2:prostate, CTV1:prostate + seminal vesicles).

The generated atlas and an example of probabilistic label are presented in Figures 1 and 4. The automatic hard segmentations were compared against the manual segmentations using the Dice Similarity Coefficient ($DSC = 2(|A \bigcap B|/(|A| \bigcup |B|))$). A leave-one-out cross validation was performed. Thus, at each iteration a single individual was extracted from the training data and used as a test. The dice score results appear summarized in Figure 6. As expected the highest areas of coincidence are shown in the bones, but also in average the bladder and rectum, which have a good contrast in the CT. Fig. 7 depicts the distribution of all those results. As table 1 summarised , some outliers bias the average result.

**Table 1.** Average Dice Score after leave one out validation. At each time one ID is extracted from the training data set and is used as the test data. CTV1: Prostate+Seminal Vesicles, CTV2: Prostate.

| ID | Bladder | Rectum | Rfemur | Lfemur | CTV1 | CTV2 |
|---|---|---|---|---|---|---|
| 1 | 0.59 | 0.70 | 0.67 | 0.69 | 0.59 | 0.54 |
| 2 | 0.48 | 0.60 | 0.88 | 0.88 | 0.52 | 0.47 |
| 3 | 0.59 | 0.32 | 0.85 | 0.74 | 0.32 | 0.68 |
| 4 | 0.83 | 0.62 | 0.90 | 0.90 | 0.79 | 0.78 |
| 5 | 0.62 | 0.72 | 0.91 | 0.90 | 0.52 | 0.59 |
| 6 | 0.82 | 0.64 | 0.89 | 0.90 | 0.72 | 0.76 |
| 7 | 0.31 | 0.06 | 0.84 | 0.77 | 0.16 | 0.23 |
| 8 | 0.72 | 0.76 | 0.90 | 0.89 | 0.61 | 0.49 |
| 9 | 0.71 | 0.65 | 0.85 | 0.80 | 0.55 | 0.68 |
| 10 | 0.76 | 0.69 | 0.81 | 0.77 | 0.77 | 0.80 |
| 11 | 0.46 | 0.52 | 0.63 | 0.64 | 0.27 | 0.27 |
| 12 | 0.36 | 0.40 | 0.90 | 0.88 | 0.36 | 0.46 |
| 13 | 0.80 | 0.77 | 0.83 | 0.88 | 0.78 | 0.78 |
| 14 | 0.79 | 0.77 | 0.89 | 0.88 | 0.70 | 0.62 |
| 15 | 0.44 | 0.64 | 0.90 | 0.87 | 0.35 | 0.32 |
| 16 | 0.78 | 0.59 | 0.86 | 0.85 | 0.59 | 0.57 |
| 17 | 0.73 | 0.78 | 0.90 | 0.86 | 0.74 | 0.72 |
| 18 | 0.90 | 0.67 | 0.86 | 0.87 | 0.77 | 0.78 |
| 19 | 0.40 | 0.20 | 0.89 | 0.87 | 0.60 | 0.55 |
| Average | 0.636 | 0.583 | 0.851 | 0.834 | 0.564 | 0.583 |
| Stdev | 0.180 | 0.202 | 0.076 | 0.076 | 0.192 | 0.177 |
| Max | 0.898 | 0.778 | 0.908 | 0.902 | 0.791 | 0.795 |
| Min | 0.315 | 0.055 | 0.629 | 0.644 | 0.161 | 0.232 |

In general a good agreement was obtained with this approach. The main cause of error in the automatic segmentation results are related to organ variation, particularly with the CTV1 (vesicles + prostate), and the prostate. Obesity appears to also be a source of error, as it induces a quite important variability to the training data set. We must consider the high interobserver variability which bias also the obtained results. This should be alleviated with the contribution of additional subjects to the atlas or with the

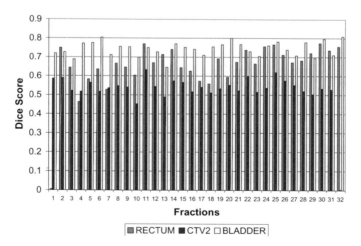

**Fig. 8.** Dice Scores for the CBCT segmentation

computation of a set of atlases to stratify subjects. This will allow to group portions of the populations that can be further mapped together in a single template.

Motivated by the potential utility of the approach for interindividual segmentation, we also tested the method to segment structures from the CBCT scans acquired during 32 fractions for one single individual. Results are summarised in Fig. 8.

## 4    Conclusion

We have presented in this paper the first step aimed at the creation of a common template for the mapping of organs at risk (OAR) as a basis to produce predictive models of toxicity. The validation of the mapping was performed by using the atlas-based segmentation results, where the OAR and prostate were delineated and compared with manual segmentations. The automatic segmentation of the prostate, rectum, bladder and femur from CT images using a probability atlas scheme had quite good correspondence with the manual segmentation, and may provide useful initial constraints for further segmentation methods, such as active contours or statistical models. We tested different levels of thresholding and selected a 50% threshold over the propagated probability maps, but in future work we want to optimize the segmentation for a particular organ of interest using improved techniques from those maps. The analysis was performed on CT and not in MRI, which would give more accuracy in terms of soft tissues registration, but the goal is to map the delivered dose from available data. We intend to perform a large voxel-wise interindividual analysis, where all the multivariate information (anatomy, dosimetry plans, toxicity) across a different population would be mapped using non rigid registration strategies.

Next step will be to compare with different non-rigid registration techniques and to relate with the inter/intra expert segmentation variability. Approaches such as STAPLE [25], will help us to assess the confidence of the ground truth and to generate robust segmentations. Further steps in Image-guided radiotherapy is the re-planning of the dose distribution during the treatment. As an exploratory way, we also obtained good agreement in organ segmentation for a single individual from the 32 CBCT scans acquired during the treatment. Future work will include dose-tracking in the tissues during the fractions and so a more accurate and adequate treatment for the patient according to the predictive models of toxicity encompassing a multivariate analysis.

## References

1. de Crevoisier, R., Tucker, S.L., Dong, L., Mohan, R., Cheung, R., Cox, J.D., Kuban, D.A.: Increased risk of biochemical and local failure in patients with distended rectum on the planning ct for prostate cancer radiotherapy. Int. J. Radiat. Oncol. Biol. Phys. 62(4), 965–973 (2005)
2. Fiorino, C., Rancati, T., Valdagni, R.: Predictive models of toxicity in external radiotherapy: dosimetric issues. Cancer 115(suppl. 13), 3135–3140 (2009)
3. Ting, J.Y., Wu, X., Fiedler, J.A., Yang, C., Watzich, M.L., Markoe, A.: Dose-volume histograms for bladder and rectum. Int. J. Radiat. Oncol. Biol. Phys. 38(5), 1105–1111 (1997)

4. Jensen, I., Carl, J., Lund, B., Larsen, E.H., Nielsen, J.: Radiobiological impact of reduced margins and treatment technique for prostate cancer in terms of tumor control probability (TCP) and normal tissue complication probability (NTCP). Med. Dosim (May 2010)

5. Cambria, R., Jereczek-Fossa, B.A., Cattani, F., Garibaldi, C., Zerini, D., Fodor, C., Serafini, F., Pedroli, G., Orecchia, R.: Evaluation of late rectal toxicity after conformal radiotherapy for prostate cancer: a comparison between dose-volume constraints and ntcp use. Strahlenther Onkol. 185(6), 384–389 (2009)

6. Grigorov, G.N., Chow, J.C.L., Grigorov, L., Jiang, R., Barnett, R.B.: IMRT: improvement in treatment planning efficiency using ntcp calculation independent of the dose-volume-histogram. Med. Phys. 33(5), 1250–1258 (2006)

7. Sohn, M., Alber, M., Yan, D.: Principal component analysis-based pattern analysis of dose-volume histograms and influence on rectal toxicity. Int. J. Radiat. Oncol. Biol. Phys. 69(1), 230–239 (2007)

8. Fiorino, C., Vavassori, V., Sanguineti, G., Bianchi, C., Cattaneo, G.M., Piazzolla, A., Cozzarini, C.: Rectum contouring variability in patients treated for prostate cancer: impact on rectum dose-volume histograms and normal tissue complication probability. Radiother. Oncol. 63(3), 249–255 (2002)

9. Fiorino, C., Cozzarini, C., Vavassori, V., Sanguineti, G., Bianchi, C., Cattaneo, G.M., Foppiano, F., Magli, A., Piazzolla, A.: Relationships between dvhs and late rectal bleeding after radiotherapy for prostate cancer: analysis of a large group of patients pooled from three institutions. Radiother. Oncol. 64(1), 1–12 (2002)

10. Marzi, S., Arcangeli, G., Saracino, B., Petrongari, M.G., Bruzzaniti, V., Iaccarino, G., Landoni, V., Soriani, A., Benassi, M.: Relationships between rectal wall dose-volume constraints and radiobiologic indices of toxicity for patients with prostate cancer. Int. J. Radiat. Oncol. Biol. Phys. 68(1), 41–49 (2007)

11. Benk, V.A., Adams, J.A., Shipley, W.U., Urie, M.M., McManus, P.L., Efird, J.T., Willett, C.G., Goitein, M.: Late rectal bleeding following combined x-ray and proton high dose irradiation for patients with stages t3-t4 prostate carcinoma. Int. J. Radiat. Oncol. Biol. Phys. 26(3), 551–557 (1993)

12. Rancati, T., Fiorino, C., Gagliardi, G., Cattaneo, G.M., Sanguineti, G., Borca, V.C., Cozzarini, C., Fellin, G., Foppiano, F., Girelli, G., Menegotti, L., Piazzolla, A., Vavassori, V., Valdagni, R.: Fitting late rectal bleeding data using different ntcp models: results from an italian multi-centric study (airopros0101). Radiother. Oncol. 73(1), 21–32 (2004)

13. Cheung, M.R., Tucker, S.L., Dong, L., de Crevoisier, R., Lee, A.K., Frank, S., Kudchadker, R.J., Thames, H., Mohan, R., Kuban, D.: Investigation of bladder dose and volume factors influencing late urinary toxicity after external beam radiotherapy for prostate cancer. Int. J. Radiat. Oncol. Biol. Phys. 67(4), 1059–1065 (2007)

14. Skala, M., Rosewall, T., Dawson, L., Divanbeigi, L., Lockwood, G., Thomas, C., Crook, J., Chung, P., Warde, P., Catton, C.: Patient-assessed late toxicity rates and principal component analysis after image-guided radiation therapy for prostate cancer. Int. J. Radiat. Oncol. Biol. Phys. 68(3), 690–698 (2007)

15. Jani, A.B., Hand, C.M., Pelizzari, C.A., Roeske, J.C., Krauz, L., Vijayakumar, S.: Biological-effective versus conventional dose volume histograms correlated with late genitourinary and gastrointestinal toxicity after external beam radiotherapy for prostate cancer: a matched pair analysis. BMC Cancer 3, 16 (2003)

16. Meijer, G.J., de Klerk, J., Bzdusek, K., van den Berg, H.A., Janssen, R., Kaus, M.R., Rodrigus, P., van der Toorn, P.P.: What ctv-to-ptv margins should be applied for prostate irradiation? four-dimensional quantitative assessment using model-based deformable image registration techniques. Int. J. Radiat. Oncol. Biol. Phys. 72(5), 1416–1425 (2008)

17. Jaffray, D.A., Lindsay, P.E., Brock, K.K., Deasy, J.O., Tomé, W.A.: Accurate accumulation of dose for improved understanding of radiation effects in normal tissue. Int. J. Radiat. Oncol. Biol. Phys. 76(suppl. 3), S135–S139 (2010)

18. Kupchak, C., Battista, J., Dyk, J.V.: Experience-driven dose-volume histogram maps of NTCP risk as an aid for radiation treatment plan selection and optimization. Med. Phys. 35(1), 333–343 (2008)

19. Heemsbergen, W.D., Al-Mamgani, A., Witte, M.G., van Herk, M., Pos, F.J., Lebesque, J.V.: Urinary obstruction in prostate cancer patients from the dutch trial (68 gy vs. 78 gy): Relationships with local dose, acute effects, and baseline characteristics. Int. J. Radiat. Oncol. Biol. Phys. (January 2010)

20. Witte, M.G., Heemsbergen, W.D., Bohoslavsky, R., Pos, F.J., Al-Mamgani, A., Lebesque, J.V., van Herk, M.: Relating dose outside the prostate with freedom from failure in the dutch trial 68 gy vs. 78 gy. Int. J. Radiat. Oncol. Biol. Phys. 77(1), 131–138 (2010)

21. Dowling, J., Fripp, J., Freer, P., Ourselin, S., Salvado, O.: Automatic atlas-based segmentation of the prostate: a miccai 2009 prostate segmentation challenge entry. In: Worskshop in Med. Image Comput. Comput. Assist. Interv., (Pt. 2), pp. 17–24 (2009)

22. Rohlfing, T., Brandt, R., Menzel, R., Maurer, C.R.: Evaluation of atlas selection strategies for atlas-based image segmentation with application to confocal microscopy images of bee brains. Neuroimage 21(4), 1428–1442 (2004)

23. Ourselin, S., Roche, A., Subsol, G., Pennec, X., Ayache, N.: Reconstructing a 3D structure from serial histological sections. Image and Vision Computing 19(1), 25–31 (2001)

24. Vercauteren, T., Pennec, X., Perchant, A., Ayache, N.: Non-parametric diffeomorphic image registration with the demons algorithm. In: Ayache, N., Ourselin, S., Maeder, A. (eds.) MICCAI 2007, Part II. LNCS, vol. 4792, pp. 319–326. Springer, Heidelberg (2007)

25. Warfield, S.K., Zou, K.H., Wells, W.M.: Simultaneous truth and performance level estimation (STAPLE): An algorithm for the validation of image segmentation. IEEE Trans. Med. Imag. 23, 903–921 (2004)

# Realtime TRUS/MRI Fusion Targeted-Biopsy for Prostate Cancer: A Clinical Demonstration of Increased Positive Biopsy Rates[*]

Samuel Kadoury[1], Pingkun Yan[1], Sheng Xu[1], Neil Glossop[2], Peter Choyke[3], Baris Turkbey[3], Peter Pinto[3], Bradford J. Wood[3], and Jochen Kruecker[1]

[1] Philips Research North America, Briarcliff Manor, NY 10510, USA
{samuel.kadoury,jochen.kruecker}@philips.com
[2] Philips Healthcare, Toronto, ON M5V 2J1, Canada
[3] National Institutes of Health, Bethesda, MD 20892, USA

**Abstract.** In this paper, a system for fusion of realtime transrectal ultrasound (TRUS) with pre-acquired 3D images of the prostate is presented with a clinical demonstration on a cohort of 101 patients with suspicion of prostate cancer. Electromagnetically tracked biopsy guides for endocavity ultrasound transducers were calibrated and used to fuse MRI-based suspicious lesion locations with ultrasound image coordinates. The prostate shape is segmented from MRI in a semi-automated fashion via a model-based approach, and intraoperative image registration is performed between MR and ultrasound image space to superimpose target fiducials markers on the ultrasound image. In order to align both modalities, a surface model is automatically extracted from 2D swept TRUS images using a partial active shape model, utilizing image features and prior statistics. An automatic prostate motion compensation algorithm can be triggered as needed. The results were used to display live TRUS images fused with spatially corresponding realtime multiplanar reconstructions (MPRs) of the MR image volume. In this study, all patients were scanned with 3T MRI and TRUS for biopsy. Clinical results show significant improvement of target visualization and of positive detection rates during TRUS-guided biopsies. It also demonstrates the feasibility of realtime MR/TRUS image fusion for out-of-gantry procedures.

## 1  Introduction

Prostate cancer is the second leading cancer among American men after skin cancer, with an incidence rate of 157/100,000 (2010) in the US and approximately 218,000 new cases diagnosed each year. It is the second leading cause of cancer death in men in the United States [1], with a mortality rate close to 32,000 every year. Successful screening and diagnosis of malignant tumors therefore

---

[*] This work was supported in part by the Intramural Research Program of the NIH Clinical Center and by a Collaborative Research and Development Agreement between NIH and Philips Healthcare.

A. Madabhushi et al. (Eds.): Prostate Cancer Imaging 2010, LNCS 6367, pp. 52–62, 2010.

becomes critical in order to treat highly suspicious cases. Towards this end, once a rectal exam and a prostate-specific antigen (PSA) test is performed, a transrectal ultrasound (TRUS) examination is scheduled. This type of procedure is the most frequently used method for image-guided biopsy and therapy of prostate cancer due to its real-time nature, low cost, and simplicity [2].

However because the accuracy of TRUS procedures for prostate cancer is rather limited, biopsies are generally not lesion-targeted. Instead, the vast majority of biopsies are carried out using 6 to 12 core systematic geometric sampling of the prostate [3]. With over a million biopsies performed annually in the US, a significant rate of false negatives was reported for sextant biopsy in particular, reaching up to 30% [4]. This stems from the fact that ultrasound prostate imaging has many limitations such as low intrinsic contrast between tumor and non-tumor on ultrasound, and very high speckle artifacts in the images. Furthermore the biopsies are carried out in an inherently undirected fashion in each zone. On the other hand potential alternatives to TRUS have been studied extensively and continue to be an active area of research.

Novel imaging methods are being sought for screening, diagnosis, and staging of prostate cancer, as well as for biopsy and therapy guidance. Advanced magnetic resonance imaging (MRI) methods such as dynamic contrast enhanced MRI (DCE-MRI) and MR spectroscopy are becoming increasingly attractive as new diagnostic modalities for prostate cancer [5,6]. The promise of advanced MR prostate imaging has also stimulated research in MR-compatible robots for biopsy or brachytherapy applications [2,7]. It is also a well suited modality for visualizing the prostate anatomy and focal lesions that are suspicious for prostate cancer. Unfortunately, MRI imaging is costly and typically not a real-time modality and due to the magnetic environment, this increases the complexity of interventional procedures, making the use of MRI for routine biopsy guidance problematic. Fusion of pre-acquired MRI with electro-magnetically tracked TRUS has therefore been investigated by several groups [8,9]. Kaplan et al. propose a TRUS/MR fusion technique in transperineal biopsy, using a stepper-stabilizer commonly used for brachytherapy [10]. Another method based on the same modalities was applied for brachytherapy [11], reporting residual errors of less than 2 mm. None of those approaches, however, offers the ease of use and flexibility of freehand TRUS needed for transrectal prostate biopsy. Lastly, very few studies have demonstrated the advantages of fusion-targeted biopsies in large-scale clinical trials.

We introduce a solution to this problem where we propose a method to segment the prostate gland from previously acquired T2-weighted MR images and fuse the 3D model to realtime TRUS images acquired in the operating room during biopsy procedure, thus exploiting the advantages of each modality [10]. To this end, key technologies in adaptive prostate segmentation, both from MRI and ultrasound data, as well as in multi-modal registration were addressed to achieve a robust, reliable and accurate fusion system. Pre-operative data processing is accomplished through a partial active shape model. Then, registration is performed in a semi-supervised fashion, where a motion compensation algorithm

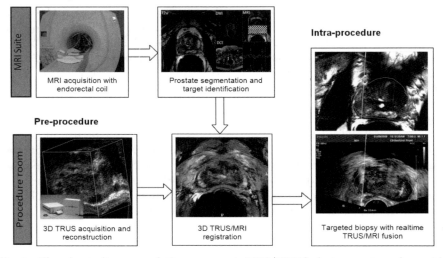

**Fig. 1.** Flowchart diagram of the proposed MRI/TRUS fusion system for guided prostate biopsy

is integrated in the guidance software to accommodate for gland and patient displacement during the procedure. In this paper, we present our overall system aimed at providing prostate fusion imaging based on technologies that require no or only minimal modification to the standard clinical workflow. The purpose of this particular study is to present the clinical relevance of such a fusion system in a routine environment with results provided from a cohort of 101 cases. The potentials of such an approach is to give access to fusion-targeted biopsies in conventional procedure room (out-of-gantry), and ultimately translate the technology to a urology office setting. Figure 1 shows the framework of registering a tracked ultrasound sequence to the pre-operative 3D image. In this scenario, we obtain a pre-operative MRI scan which is used to segment the shape of the prostate with annotated target lesion landmarks. Once the patient is positioned, a TRUS image sequence of the prostate is recorded and processed for a volume reconstruction. We use this data to segment the prostate from TRUS, and apply a surface-based registration algorithm for MRI/TRUS fusion. The guidance platform helps radiologists track the targeted tumor for targeted biopsy, with the option of referring to the prior MRI to sample suspicious tissue. Inherent tracking errors due to distortions in the magnetic field from metallic instruments are reduced by the proposed image-based solution which provides image fusion by the same tracked US probe. The advantage of using MRI data is the high resolution 3D image where the suspicious lesions can be easily visualized before or during the intervention. The paper is organized as follows. Section 2 presents the hardware setup, prostate model segmentation and multi-modal registration algorithms. In Section 3 we present our clinical results and the relevance of using such a method. Finally, the last section brings a perspective to the paper with future enhancements.

## 2   Method

### 2.1   System Setup

Figure 2 shows the set up of the system. 3D images are acquired on a Philips 3T Achieva MR scanner (Philips Medical Systems, Best, The Netherlands), collected with an endorectal coil. The US guidance experiment was carried out using the 2nd generation Aurora electro-magnetic tracking system (Northern Digital Inc, NDI, Waterloo, ON, Canada). A tracking field generator is mounted near the operating table using an articulated arm by D&K Technologies (Barum, Germany). A Philips iU22 ultrasound scanner was used for real-time guidance and the ultrasound images were captured using a frame-grabber card (Winnov USA, Santa Clara, CA) at 30 fps. The software platform used was a JAVA-based interventional navigation software previously demonstrated for radiofrequency ablation (RFA). Target lesion identification is performed by a radiologist prior to intervention on T2-weighted (T2w) images. SENSE protocols were used for most scans, in accordance with the clinical scan protocol used.

### 2.2   Model-Based Prostate Segmentation from MRI

Once the T2w MR images of the patient's prostate is acquired, a deformable model is used to segment the prostate by using the boundary features and statistical shape models. A given image is segmented when the associated energy of the deformable contour is minimized. The energy function is defined as:

$$E = E_f + E_s \tag{1}$$

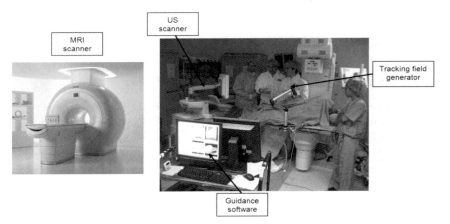

**Fig. 2.** System setup in the operating room with tracking device

where $E_f$ denotes the content-based filtering response energy term and $E_s$ is the constrain added to the energy term which is derived from the prostate shape statistics. In our work, the feature energy term $E_f$ is defined by the multi-scale gradient magnitudes at the contour points. The prostate shape statistics is computed by using an active shape model (ASM) [12]. The obtained shape statistics consists of a mean shape $\bar{s}$ and a set of eigenshapes $\phi = \{e_i | i \in [1, N]\}$. After initializing the segmentation by putting the mean shape $\bar{s}$ on an image $I$, the iterative energy minimization strategy used in ASM [12] is adopted to segment the image. The associated energy function (1) is minimized in two steps during each iteration. First, the feature term is minimized by moving each contour point along the normal directions of the deformable contour to a location with the largest feature response. A new model $S'_{MR}$ with a smallest feature energy $E_f$ is thus obtained. Then, the shape statistics is used to constrain the newly updated deformable model as $\hat{S}_{MR} = \phi \mathbf{b}^T$. The iterative minimization continues until the deformation converges towards a minimum or the maximal number of allowed iterations is reached. The final shape contour $\hat{S}_{MR}$ is considered as the segmentation result. The method is a semi-supervised approach where the level of accuracy varies on the user's expertise and time requirements to obtain a precise representation. Figure 3 illustrate an example of this process.

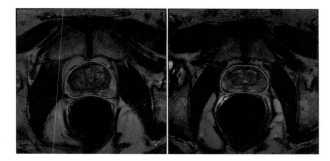

**Fig. 3.** Sample segmentation results of the prostate from MRI. The ground truth is shown in red and the obtained model-based segmentation result is displayed in green.

### 2.3    TRUS Image Segmentation

A 3D ultrasound volume is obtained by sweeping the 2D TRUS probe across the prostate. Automatic prostate segmentation in TRUS images is highly desired in this case so to alleviate the manual interventions. Unfortunately, robust and automated prostate segmentation is challenging due to low contrast and missing boundaries in shadow areas caused by calcifications or hyperdense prostate tissues. We apply a method we previously presented which uses a priori shapes estimated from partial contours for segmenting the prostate boundaries [13].

The method is able to automatically extract prostate boundary from 2D TRUS images without user interaction for shape correction in shadow areas. At its core, shape statistics of the prostate are computed using a point distribution model (PDM). However, in order to deal with missing boundaries in shadow areas, contours are estimated by using a partial active shape model (PASM), which takes partial contours as input but returns a complete shape estimation such that the model is formulated as:

$$\hat{S_{US}} = \bar{S_{US}} + \mathbf{\Phi b}_s \tag{2}$$

with mean shape $\bar{S_{US}}$ and a matrix $\mathbf{\Phi}$, which includes the most significant top eigenvectors of the input data covariance matrix. On the other hand to accommodate for salient contours, $\mathbf{b}_s$ is the coefficient vector based on partial salient training data. With this previous shape guidance defined in (2), an optimal search is performed to minimize the energy functional related to the deformable model:

$$E(v_i) = E_{ext}(v_i) + E_{int}(v_i) + E_{PASM}(v_i) \tag{3}$$

where the external energy $E_{ext}(v_i)$ is defined by the contrast of feature vectors detecting contrast variations, the internal energy $E_{int}(v_i)$ represents the model continuity and curvature, used to preserve the geometric shape. Finally, the PASM term $E_{PASM}(v_i)$ is defined by the distance between the model and corresponding active points. For image segmentation, efficient dynamic programming in a multi-resolution approach is adopted. The level of accuracy of the proposed approach is evaluated at $2.01 \pm 1.02$mm on a cohort of 19 patients [13].

## 2.4   Surface-Based TRUS/MRI Registration

MRI/TRUS fusion requires real-time image registration between the two datasets. In our protocol, the registration is conducted at the beginning of the ultrasound procedure, so the physician can use the time during the computation to examine the patient sonographically. The registration can be described by the following chain of transformations, progressing from the US image towards the MRI:

$$\mathbf{T}_{US \to MRI} = \mathbf{T}_{3DUS \to MRI} \cdot \mathbf{T}_{2.5DUS \to 3DUS} \cdot \mathbf{T}_{US \to 2.5DUS} \tag{4}$$

where $\mathbf{T}_{US \to 2.5DUS}$ is the transformation from the ultrasound image space to the local coordinate system of the tracking sensors attached to the ultrasound probe, $\mathbf{T}_{2.5DUS \to 3DUS}$ is the real-time tracking data of the ultrasound probe and $\mathbf{T}_{3DUS \to MRI}$ is the registration transformation we seek between the patient and the localizer. Since the probe is spatially tracked, the reconstructed ultrasound volume is inherently registered to the tracking space. Therefore the cost function which optimizes the parameters of $T$, namely $t$ and $R$ follows an ICP-like objective:

$$E = \underset{\mathbf{T}_{3DUS \to MRI}}{\text{argmin}} \sum_{i \in S_{US}} [(Rp_i + t - q_i) \cdot n_i]^2 \tag{5}$$

which minimizes the alignment of both point sets from the prior MRI and TRUS segmented model, with $q_i \in S_{MR}$ and $n_i$ defined as the normal at each point coordinate of the MRI model. Although not a perfectly accurate method, the observed prostate deformation caused by the ultrasound transducer can be controlled by the applied probe pressure to obtain a shape similar to the deformation caused by the endorectal coil used during MRI. Registration is performed by rigidly aligning both shapes for accurate mapping of MR targets in the TRUS images.

### 2.5   Intra-operative Motion Compensation

Involuntarily patient motion due to pain or probe pressure related to the needle insertion may cause the prostate to shift from its originally swept position. In addition, the transrectal probe can itself move and distort the prostate, while the patients respiratory motion may slightly deviate the gland from its original location [14]. Therefore, to maintain image fusion from these artifacts, realtime image-based motion compensation can be triggered by the user to correct the registration intraoperatively. Since the ultrasound images are acquired from a tracked probe, mapping the slice back to the 3D volume is a viable solution. However, single slice volume registration is very sensitive to input noise. There are indeed many local minima along the off-plane direction which can offset the registration. Hence we propose a method using multiple image frames for the compensation [15], where a subset of frames demonstrating significant differences in translation and rotation are selected. The registration between these frames and the reference ultrasound volume can be considered as 2.5D to 3D registration. The objective function is given by:

$$O(R,t) = \sum_{k=1}^{N} \sum_{(x,y)} [I_k(x,y) - V(T_k(x,y,0))]^2 \tag{6}$$

where $N$ is the number of frames used in the registration adjustment, $I_k$ is the $k^{th}$ 2D frame, $V$ is the reference ultrasound volume, and $T_k$ is a transformation model between $I_k$ and $V$ with a parameter vector $k$. Since the 2.5D image acquisition is performed at a high frame-rate, the relative prostate motion between the selected ultrasound frames is negligible. In the example illustrated in Figure 4, we see the

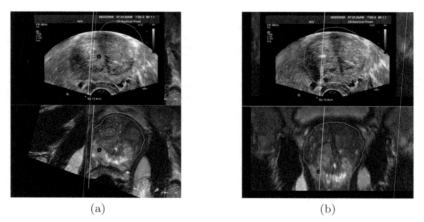

(a)                                                    (b)

**Fig. 4.** Motion compensation results (a) before and (b) after realignment

updated fusion after using four ultrasound image frames which were registered to the reference ultrasound volume.

# 3    Clinical Experiments

The proposed targeted-fusion system was used and validated in a clinical study incorporating patients with suspicion of prostate cancer. We tested the approach by comparing results with standard measures used for prostate biopsies. Study design and results are presented in this section.

## 3.1    Biopsy Protocol

The patient studies were carried out at the National Institutes of Health Clinical Center to evaluate the system's performance under an IRB approved protocol, with written informed consent from each patient. In all, 101 patients were enrolled in this study and inclusion criteria consisted of a PSA > 2.5 or an abnormal digital rectal exam. At least 1 lesion suspicious for prostate cancer had to be present on the MRI. The mean age was 61.7 (range 41 - 81) and median age of 61. The mean PSA was 8.3 (range 0.21 - 103) and median of 5.4. From all the patients who were enrolled in this study, 60 had at least one prior biopsy. From these, 26 had a negative prior biopsy and 34 had a positive prior biopsy.

Four sequences were acquired for each patient: T2w (axial, sagittal, coronal), DWI, DCE and MRS. The suspicious lesion locations were identified on T2w images. For each lesion, an assignment of suspicion label based on low, moderate, high was performed.

## 3.2    Results

All patients were under general anesthesia and were first treated with conventional TRUS-guided 12-core double-sextant biopsy. This was then followed by the proposed MRI-TRUS fusion-guided targeted biopsy approach with 2 cores per target (axial, sagittal view). Figure 5 shows some results of fused MRI/TRUS image guidance with US overlaid targets initially identified on the MRI.

We compared positive biopsy core rates for both sextant and targeted biopsy cores using the proposed system (Figure 6). All patients were divided in one of the following 3 categories: low, moderate and high suspicion. Biopsy rates are calculated by the number of positive biopsy cores divided by the total number of cores in each category. We can observe biopsy rates are nearly identical in low-suspicion patients (6.5%), while in the two other categories, there is a significant increase in positive rates. Moreover, this increase is even more pronounced for targeted biopsies, whereas the sextant core rate increase by a factor of 3.7 between high and low suspicion patients, the factors is 6.5 for targeted cores. Furthermore, the targeted core rate is significantly higher than the core rate ($p < 0.001$) in all categories except low suspicion patients. In order to correlate the fusion-targeted procedure results with a recognized prostate cancer classification score, we computed Gleason scores obtained in the targeted lesions, where

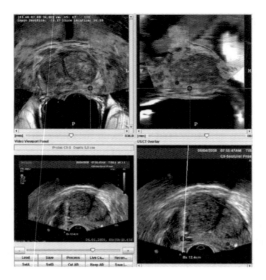

**Fig. 5.** Registration of MRI/TRUS for image guidance, fusing T2w MRI fused with reference ultrasound volume (color map), along with the real-time ultrasound and target information

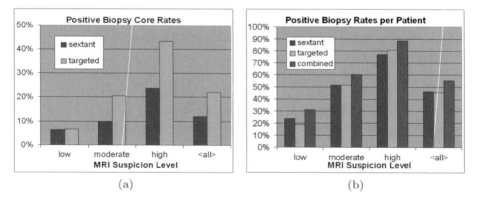

(a)                                        (b)

**Fig. 6.** Comparison of sextant vs. image fusion-targeted biopsies. (a) Biopsy core rates in low, moderate, high suspicion. (b) Biopsy core rates in low, moderate, high suspicion per patients with combined approach.

the results displayed in Figure 7 show mean values and $\pm 1$ standard deviation. We see a significant increase ($p < 0.05$) with target suspicion level, from 6.3 and 6.8 for low/moderate suspicion targets, indicative of low to moderate risk cancer, up to 7.9, indicative of high risk of cancer.

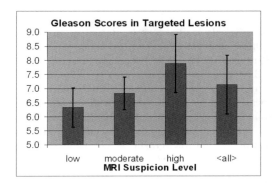

**Fig. 7.** Analysis of Gleason scores in targeted lesions

## 4 Discussion and Future Work

We have described an interventional navigation system fusing prior MRI with TRUS for image guidance. The system is used for targeted prostate biopsy and can be extended to focal therapy. Real-time fusion of MRI and ultrasound images is possible despite the presence of prostate motion. Results show that MRI-based suspicion labels correlate with both with biopsy core rates and Gleason scores. While the system has been proven to be a significant improvement to standard sextant biopsies, deformation of the prostate during MR and TRUS scans was identified as the primary source of error. Hence, deformable registration algorithms are being investigated to compensate for probe pressure in peripheral regions which modifies the prostate appearance. In conclusion, fusion-targeted biopsy potentially enables more accurate biopsy and improved patient management, in particular for patients with potential cancer and after failed sextant biopsy. Future trials in external clinical centers and out-of-gantry context are being planned for further validation.

## References

1. Jemal, A., Siegel, R., Ward, E., Murray, T., Xu, J., Thun, M.: Cancer statistics, 2007. CA: a cancer journal for clinicians 57, 43 (2007)
2. Fichtinger, G., Krieger, A., Susil, R., Tanacs, A., Whitcomb, L., Atalar, E.: Transrectal prostate biopsy inside closed MRI scanner with remote actuation, under real-time image guidance. In: Dohi, T., Kikinis, R. (eds.) MICCAI 2002. LNCS, vol. 2488, pp. 91–98. Springer, Heidelberg (2002)
3. Babaian, R., Toi, A., Kamoi, K., Troncoso, P., Sweet, J., Evans, R., Johnston, D., Chen, M.: A comparative analysis of sextant and extended 11-core multisite directed biospy strategy. J. Urol. 163, 1527 (2000)
4. Rabbani, F., Stroumbakis, N., Kava, B., Cookson, M., Fair, W.: Incidence and clinical significance of false-negative sextant prostate biopsies. J. Urol. 159, 1247–1250 (1998)

5. van Dorsten, F., van der Graaf, M., Engelbrecht, M., van Leenders, G., Verhofs-tad, A., Rijpkema, M., de la Rosette, J., Barentsz, J., Heerschap, A.: Combined quantitative dynamic contrast-enhanced MR imaging and (1)H MR spectroscopic imaging of human prostate cancer. J. Magn. Reson. Imaging 20, 250–279 (2004)
6. Kim, J., Hong, S., Choi, Y., Park, S., Ahn, H., Kim, C., Cho, K.: Wash-in rate on the basis of dynamic contrastenhanced MRI: usefulness for prostate cancer detection and localization. J. Magn. Reson. Imaging 22, 639–646 (2005)
7. Krieger, A., Csoma, C., Iordachital, I., Guion, P., Singh, A., Fichtinger, G., Whit-comb, L.: Design and preliminary accuracy studies of an MRI-guided transrectal prostate intervention system. In: Ayache, N., Ourselin, S., Maeder, A. (eds.) MIC-CAI 2007, Part II. LNCS, vol. 4792, pp. 59–67. Springer, Heidelberg (2007)
8. Hu, Y., Ahmed, H., Allen, C., Pendse, D., Sahu, M., Emberton, M., Hawkes, D., Barratt, D.: MR to ultrasound image registration for guiding prostate biopsy and interventions. In: Yang, G.-Z., Hawkes, D., Rueckert, D., Noble, A., Taylor, C. (eds.) MICCAI 2009. LNCS, vol. 5761, pp. 787–794. Springer, Heidelberg (2009)
9. Martin, S., Baumann, M., Daanen, V., Troccaz, J.: MR prior based automatic segmentation of the prostate in TRUS images for MR/TRUS data fusion. In: Proc. ISBI, pp. 640–643 (2010)
10. Kaplan, I., Oldenburg, N., Meskell, P., Blake, M., Church, P., Holupka, E.: Real time MRI-ultrasound image guided stereotactic prostate biopsy. Magn. Reson. Imaging 20, 295–299 (2002)
11. Reynier, C., Troccaz, J., Fourneret, P., Dusserre, A., Gay-Jeune, C., Descotes, J., Bolla, M., Giraud, J.: MRI/TRUS data fusion for prostate brachytherapy. Prelim-inary results. Med. Phys. 31, 1568–1575 (2004)
12. Cootes, T., Taylor, C., Cooper, D., Graham, J.: Active shape models - their training and application. CVIU 61, 38–59
13. Yan, P., Xu, S., Turkbey, B., Kruecker, J.: Discrete deformable model guided by partial active shape model for TRUS image segmentation. IEEE T. Biomed. Eng. 57, 1158–1166 (2010)
14. Malone, S., Crook, J., Kendal, W., Szanto, J.: Respiratory induced prostate motion: quantification and characterization. Int. J. Radiat. Oncol. Biol. Phys. 48, 105–109 (2000)
15. Xu, S., Kruecker, J., Turkbey, B., Glossop, N., Singh, A., Choyke, P., Pinto, P., Wood, B.J.: Real-time MRI-TRUS fusion for guidance of targeted prostate biopsies. Comput. Aided Surg. 13, 255–264 (2008)

# HistoCAD: Machine Facilitated Quantitative Histoimaging with Computer Assisted Diagnosis

John E. Tomaszewski

Hospital at the University of Pennsylvania, Pennsylvania, USA

## 1 Abstract

Prostatic adenocarcinoma (CAP) is the most common malignancy in American men. In 2010 there will be an estimated 217,730 new cases and 32,050 deaths from CAP in the US. The diagnosis of prostatic adenocarcinoma is made exclusively from the histological evaluation of prostate tissue. The sampling protocols used to obtain 18 gauge (1.5 mm diameter) needle cores are standard sampling templates consisting of 6-12 cores performed in the context of an elevated serum value for prostate specific antigen (PSA). In this context, the prior probability of cancer is somewhat increased. However, even in this screened population, the efficiency of finding cancer is low at only approximately 20%. Histopathologists are faced with the task of reviewing the 5-10 million cores of tissue resulting from approximately 1,000,000 biopsy procedures yearly, parsing all the benign scenes from the worrisome scenes, and deciding which of the worrisome images are cancer.

All prostate cancer is not biologically the same. Some cancers are progressive despite therapy and eventually kill the patient. Other cancers are indolent. Our ability to separate aggressive from indolent cancer is good but limited to population statistics describing the distribution of features such as tumor size, tumor stage, PSA value, and tumor grade. The Gleason grading system of CAP is the single most powerful feature for the prediction of outcome in CAP. The Gleason grading system recognizes 5 basic architectural patterns which structurally describe a disturbance of normal inter-glandular organizational relationships on a 2-10 scoring scale. The bins of score 6 or less; score 7; and score 8 or more have significantly different biological outcomes in meta-analysis. In assigning Gleason grade the accurate identification of Gleason patterns 4 and 5 is the most important task for the histopathologist. Inter-observer variance in the recognition of Gleason patterns 4/5 is an important limitation in grading. Educational programs can improve concordance across labs.

Machine facilitated quantitative histoimaging with computer assisted diagnosis (HistoCAD) offers an algorithmic classifier approach to Gleason grading with the promise of near 100% reproducibility. Recent improvements in virtual slide scanning technology allow for ready access to whole slide digital images on which to focus computational solutions. There are, however, many challenges to effective HistoCAD programs.

The size of the data is enormous in comparison to other diagnostic modalities. A high resolution CT scan comprises $512 \times 512 \times 512$ spatial elements, or 134

A. Madabhushi et al. (Eds.): Prostate Cancer Imaging 2010, LNCS 6367, pp. 63–65, 2010.

million voxels. A single core of prostate tissue digitized at 40X magnification is approximately $15,000 \times 15,000$ elements, or 225 million pixels. Most biopsy procedures generate 12 cores or 2.7 billion pixels per patient investigation! Computational efficiency in dealing with data sets of this size is critical.

Finding a strong representation of the cancer in a whole slide image is a crucial first task of any HistoCAD algorithm. Our collaborative group at Rutgers University and the University of Pennsylvania has studied two approaches. Monaco et al [1] has reported on the high-throughput detection of prostatic cancer in whole mount histological sections using probabilistic pairwise Markov models. In this method, gland lumens are segmented, and then the gland areas are extracted. The classification of individual glands leverages two features: (1) cancerous glands tend to be smaller than benign glands, and (2) cancerous (benign) glands tend to be in proximity to other cancerous (benign) glands. This last feature describes a spatial dependency which was modeled using a Markov prior which encourages neighboring glands to share the same label. Finally, the algorithm consolidates the malignant glands in contiguous regions using the distance hull algorithm. The net effect is to quickly capture malignancy enriched areas with 87% sensitivity and a false positive rate of only 10%. Such regions of interest are ideal targets for molecular analyses or second set image queries.

A second approach to cancer detection which has been studied by our group is employs a boosted Baysesian multi-resolution classifier for prostate cancer detection from digitized needle biopsies [2]. This algorithm decomposes the whole slide image into an image pyramid composed of multiple resolution levels. Features are then extracted which include first order statistics, co-occurrence features and Gabor features. Regions are identified as being cancer by using a boosted Bayesian classifier on a multi-resolution framework such that regions identified as cancer via the classifier at lower resolution levels are subsequently examined in greater detail at higher resolution levels, thereby allowing for the rapid and efficient analysis of large images. This process models the approach of expert histopathologists in gleaning information at different scales in the diagnostic process.

The density of HistoCAD data offers the potential power of interrogating the histoimages with large multidimensional feature sets. Object level features addressing structure such as size and shape, texture, chromatin, as well as spatial arrangement features such as Voronoi tessellation, Delaunay triangulation, and minimum spanning trees can create thousands of dimensions of features. Graph theory can be used to model prostate cancer grades. Spatial arrangement features offer a series of descriptors which capture the size, shape, and arrangement of gland structures related to nuclei [3]. To date such approaches have been used to reproduce expert annotations of grade allowing for the possibilities of improved quality of grading and the consideration of high throughput, grade-stratified molecular analyses. The next steps will be to extend these methods to the discovery of value added structural features which provide informative data beyond Gleason grading which could be used in the modeling of disease progression and response to therapy.

Finally, the hypothesis that quantitative high resolution image data represents an integrated statement across genome, transcriptome, proteome and epigenome can be explored using HistoCAD. The fusion of HistoCAD data molecular data streams may provide a powerful paradigm for precision medicine.

# References

1. Monaco, J.P., Tomaszewski, J.E., Feldman, M.D., Hagemann, I., Moradi, M., Mousavi, P., Boag, A., Davidson, C., Abolmaesumi, P., Madabhushi, A.: High-throughput detection of prostate cancer in histological sections using probabilistic pairwise markov models. Medical Image Analysis 14(4), 617–629 (2010)
2. Doyle, S., Feldman, M., Tomaszewski, J., Madabhushi, A.: A boosted bayesian multi-resolution classifier for prostate cancer detection from digitized needle biopsies. IEEE Transactions on Biomedical Engineering (2010) (in press)
3. Doyle, S., Hwang, M., Shah, K., Madabhushi, A., Feldman, M., Tomaszeweski, J.: Automated grading of prostate cancer using architectural and textural image features. In: 4th IEEE International Symposium on Biomedical Imaging: From Nano to Macro, ISBI 2007, pp. 1284–1287 (2007)

# Registration of *In Vivo* Prostate Magnetic Resonance Images to Digital Histopathology Images

A.D. Ward[1], C. Crukley[6], C. McKenzie[1,2,6], J. Montreuil[1], E. Gibson[1,3],
J.A. Gomez[4], M. Moussa[4], G. Bauman[5], and A. Fenster[1,2,6]

[1] Robarts Research Institute
ward@robarts.ca
[2] Department of Medical Biophysics,
[3] Biomedical Engineering Graduate Program,
[4] Department of Pathology,
[5] Department of Oncology,
The University of Western Ontario, London, Ontario, Canada
[6] Lawson Health Research Institute, London, Ontario, Canada

**Abstract.** Early and accurate diagnosis of prostate cancer enables minimally invasive therapies to cure the cancer with less morbidity. The purpose of this work is to non-rigidly register *in vivo* pre-prostatectomy prostate medical images to regionally-graded histopathology images from post-prostatectomy specimens, seeking a relationship between the multi parametric imaging and cancer distribution and aggressiveness. Our approach uses image-based registration in combination with a magnetically tracked probe to orient the physical slicing of the specimen to be parallel to the *in vivo* imaging planes, yielding a tractable 2D registration problem. We measured a target registration error of 0.85 mm, a mean slicing plane marking error of 0.7 mm, and a mean slicing error of 0.6 mm; these results compare favourably with our 2.2 mm diagnostic MR image thickness. Qualitative evaluation of *in vivo* imaging-histopathology fusion reveals excellent anatomic concordance between MR and digital histopathology.

## 1 Introduction

Prostate cancer is the most common non-cutaneous cancer in men and kills more than 600 men in the United States and Canada each week [1,2]. One out of every seven men will develop prostate cancer over the course of his lifetime, and one in 27 men will die of it [1]. Early prostate cancer detection increases the number of suitable treatment options and improves survival rates [3]. Although prostate biopsy is the current standard for diagnosing prostate cancer, there is substantial evidence of both overestimation and underestimation of cancer severity based on biopsy, which can lead to mismanagement of treatment. In a study of 464 patients, biopsy underestimated the true cancer severity determined after prostatectomy in 29.1% of cases, and overestimated it in 14% of cases [4].

A. Madabhushi et al. (Eds.): Prostate Cancer Imaging 2010, LNCS 6367, pp. 66–76, 2010.

It is clear that innovative advancements in technologies supporting the diagnosis and staging of prostate cancer are necessary and will have a high impact on disease management and the determination of the appropriate treatment (e.g. whether prostatectomy, with frequent side effects of impotence and incontinence, is required). The combination of multiple imaging modalities is showing great potential for the detection and localization of clinically significant prostate cancer [5]. However, the validation of imaging modalities and systems for computer-aided diagnosis requires an accurate spatial mapping between *in vivo* medical images and digital pathology images, wherein the ground truth information about cancer aggressiveness and distribution in the gland is known. This mapping is challenging to compute due to deformations applied to the prostate during *in vivo* imaging (e.g. due to the endorectal coil and transrectal ultrasound transducer), as well as differential distortion of prostate tissue during formalin fixation and histological processing.

The work presented in this paper is part of a study wherein radical prostatectomy patients provide a set of *in vivo* prostate images, with modalities including multi-parametric magnetic resonance (MR), dynamic contrast-enhanced computed tomography (CT), three-dimensional (3D) ultrasound (US), and 18F-choline positron emission tomography (PET). After removal, the prostate is histologically processed and the resulting slides are digitized at high resolution. Our high-level goal is then to non-rigidly register all of these images into a common coordinate space so that the multimodality imaging can be correlated to ground truth cancer aggressiveness and distribution assessments on digital histopathology. This correlation can then potentially be used for improved image guidance of prostate biopsy systems, e.g. [6,7,8], as well as focal therapeutic ablation modalities such as cryo, laser, radio frequency, radiation, and high-intensity focused ultrasound [9], or enable minimally invasive surgical techniques such as robot-assisted laparoscopic prostatectomy.

*The overall objective of the work described in this paper is to develop and evaluate a novel technique for the fusion, via image registration, of in vivo prostate MR images to corresponding digital pathology images.* Sub-objectives: (1) To develop and evaluate new software and hardware technology for orienting the physical slicing of the prostate to be parallel to the *in vivo* MR imaging planes, reducing the complexity of the registration problem from a 3D problem to a two-dimensional (2D) problem; and (2) to develop and use novel fiducial markers for the prostate, visible on medical images as well as digital pathology images.

Our approach centers on the use of a tracked probe to co-register fiducial markers visible on an *ex vivo* prostate image with the same markers visible on the specimen surface. Coupled with an *in vivo* to *ex vivo* image registration, this allows the determination and physical marking of the desired cutting plane from the *in vivo* image in the space of the physical specimen; we then use a specialized tool to cut along the plane defined by the markers. Previous approaches to orienting specimen slicing involve reorienting and reimaging the specimen in the MR bore until a desired imaging plane orientation is obtained [10], or making individual, per-specimen blade-guiding molds based on a segmentation of the surgical resection margins on *in vivo* MR images [11]. Our approach is novel in contrast to [10] in that we support any *in vivo* orientation of the patient, and unlike [11], we do not make the assumptions that the size, shape, and mechanical properties of the *in vivo* and formalin-fixed specimens are similar, and that the surgical resection margins can be reliably segmented on *in vivo* MR images prior to surgery. Additionally, the spherical fiducial markers used in [10] require very careful placement in order to ensure that they will lie within the pathology images. In contrast, we have developed novel strand-shaped fiducial markers that are visible on *ex vivo* imaging as well as on all pathology images. We have developed a means of nondestructively inserting these markers into the specimen and also mounting them to the specimen surface, permitting the use of a large number of markers richly describing surface deformations.

It is important to note that the work in this paper is currently being applied within the typical clinical context where our prostate specimens are from cancer patients who require follow-up diagnosis, and regulations dictate that most of the tissue remains on file. There is therefore a spacing of 5 mm between each of our histopathology images; this spacing introduces a significant challenge to an alternative approach consisting of reconstructing a 3D volume from the 2D histopathology images and then using conventional nonrigid 3D registration methods to register it to the in vivo context. Although such an approach would be applicable in the atypical research context where specimens are serially sectioned (i.e. the entire specimen is step-sectioned at 4 micron increments, yielding zero spacing between histopathology images), our work intends to address the challenges associated with translation to the clinical scenario.

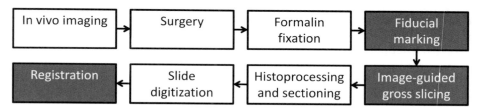

**Fig. 1.** Block diagram showing the high-level procedure conducted in this work. The dark-shaded boxes indicate the steps that are the focus of this paper. Our novel approach to fiducial marking is described in section 2.2. The use of these fiducials for image-guided gross slicing is described in section 2.3, and our registration method is given in section 2.4.

## 2   Materials and Methods

### 2.1   Overall Process

The high-level process followed in this work is described in figure 1. With institutional review board approval, we have collected image data for the first 12 of our 36 subjects. Relevant to this paper, we collect *in vivo* T2-weighted MR images

(2D FSE, TR 6050 ms, TE: 163 ms, bandwidth +/-31.25 kHz, 2 averages, FOV 14 cm, 2.20 mm thick slices, 384x256 matrix, 40 slices) using an endorectal coil surrounded by a sheath filled with barium. This configuration improves diagnostic image quality, but the inflated sheath causes deformation of the prostate. After prostatectomy, formalin fixation, and fiducial marking (described in section 2.2), T2-weighted (3D FSE, TR 2000 ms, TE 148.5 ms, bandwidth +/- 125 kHz, 3 averages, FOV 14 cm, 0.4 mm thick slices, 320x192 matrix, 160 slices) and T1-weighted (3D Spoiled Gradient Echo, TR 6.5 ms, TE 2.5 ms, flip angle 15 degrees, bandwidth +/-31.25 kHz, 8 averages, FOV 14 cm, 0.4 mm thick slices, 256x192 matrix, 160 slices) *ex vivo* MR images are taken with the specimen immersed in Christo-Lube (Lubrication Technology Inc., USA) in order to yield a black background while minimizing boundary artifacts in the MR images. The apex of the specimen is then removed by making a single cut through the prostate using the image-guided approach described in section 2.3. The remainder of the specimen is placed within an agar block for gross slicing into 5 mm thick slabs using a deli slicer, in an orientation parallel to the apex slice. The slabs are then processed using the standard paraffin embedding technique, yielding hematoxylin and eosin stained microscope slides, each containing a single 4 micron-thick section of tissue taken from the face of each slab. These slides are scanned at 0.5 micron resolution using a Tissuescope scanner (Biomedical Photometrics Inc., Canada), yielding 2D colour digital images of the sections. These images are then registered to their corresponding *in vivo* MR images using the procedure described in section 2.4.

## 2.2   Fiducial Markers

Fiducial markers used for the purpose of specimen slicing orientation and imaging-to-histopathology registration must satisfy four criteria: (1) they must appear and be localizable on *ex vivo* MR images, (2) they must appear and be localizable on digital histopathology images (e.g. they must survive physical handling, cutting, and chemical treatment during histological processing), (3) they must not disrupt tissue cutting or histological processing (e.g. they must be soft enough that they will not score/scratch the tissue during sectioning), (4) they must not damage the tissue or in any way disrupt the pathologists' interpretation. This last criterion is especially important in the context of our study since our prostates are clinical specimens, and our pathologists need to provide an accurate diagnosis of any cancer appearing at the prostate margins as this is important to patients' follow-up care. The fiducial markers described in this section have been assessed by two pathologists and deemed to be entirely non-disruptive to their assessments of these prostate specimens.

We have developed both internal and surface-mounted strand-shaped fiducial markers that fulfil these criteria. Our internal fiducial markers are made from cotton embroidery floss, soaked in a 1:40 mixture of Magnevist (Bayer AG, Germany) and blue Tissue Marking Dye (Triangle Biomedical Sciences Inc., USA).

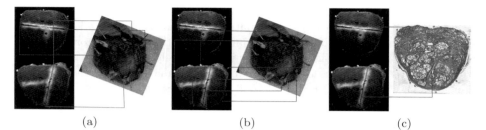

(a)                          (b)                          (c)

**Fig. 2.** (a-b) Illustration of corresponding fiducial markers on T1-weighted *ex vivo* MR images and on the specimen. (a) Two internal fiducial strands. (b) Seven surface-mounted fiducial strands. (c) Cross sectional view of fiducial markers on digital histopathology. Surface-mounted strands can be seen as small circular cross sections immediately outside of the boundary. Arrows indicate the appearance of the inked holes created by the internal fiducial strands, and their approximate corresponding locations in the MR images.

We insert these strands through the specimens with minimal tissue disruption using an 18-gauge spinal cannula with a Quincke-type point (BD Medical Inc., USA); the tip of this cannula is designed to cleanly separate tissue without any tissue removal, thus minimally disrupting the pathologists' view of the tissue at the fiducial location under the microscope. The Magnevist in the mixture results in straightforward localization of the strands on T1-weighted *ex vivo* MR images (figure 2). Since the strands would be disruptive to tissue cutting, they are removed prior to slicing, but the blue tissue ink leaves a coloured track indicating their location (figure 2(c)). Our surface-mounted fiducial markers are created by taking biopsies of lamb kidney cortex using a 16-gauge biopsy needle, which is the type that is typically used for human breast biopsy. The resulting strands are infused for 15 minutes in a 1:40 mixture of Magnevist and formalin, and attached to the prostate surface in the apex-base direction using Loctite 411 toughened, heat-resistant, ethyl cyanoacrylate adhesive (Henkel Inc., Germany). Figure 2 illustrates the appearance of these surface-mounted strands on *ex vivo* MR images and digital histopathology images. Our experience with many different adhesives and strand materials suggests that: (1) animal tissue is an ideal fiducial material since, as organic material, it adheres to positively-charged microscope slides during histological processing, (2) lamb kidney in particular has the desired softness characteristic to avoid disruption of the tissue cutting process, and (3) the choice of adhesive is important; Loctite 411 is toughened to withstand the harsh chemical and temperature environment of histological processing without hardening to the extent that it disrupts tissue cutting. These fiducials capture the deformations both at the boundary and within the gland that result from slicing and chemical processing of the tissue. Additionally, the exit points of the internal fiducial strands are used as corresponding points in the landmark-based registration depicted in figure 3(a).

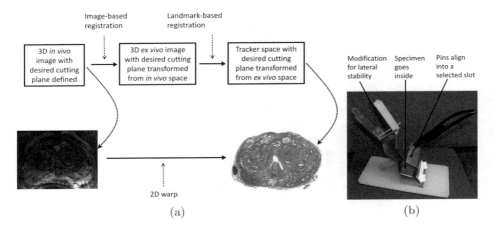

**Fig. 3.** (a) Our approach to image-guided gross slicing. (b) The ProCUT slotted forceps, used to make the first specimen cut. We designed and affixed to the device a set of steel lateral support posts in order to eliminate relative lateral motion of the upper and lower halves of the forceps.

## 2.3   Image Guidance for Specimen Slicing Orientation

A high-level overview of the specimen slice orientation procedure proposed in this work is given in figure 3(a). We begin with the selection of a desired *in vivo* MR imaging plane along which we wish to make the first specimen cut. The T2-weighted *in vivo* MR image is then rigidly registered to the T2-weighted *ex vivo* MR image using a manual alignment followed by a refinement, if necessary, using an automated block matching technique [12]. The transformation given by this registration places the desired cutting plane into the coordinate system of the *ex vivo* image. The exit points of the internal fiducial markers are then localized in the *ex vivo* image using interactive software, and on the specimen surface using a probe tracked by an Aurora magnetic tracking system (Northern Digital Inc., Canada). These corresponding points permit a rigid, landmark-based transformation of the desired cutting plane into the space of the magnetic tracker. Using software developed in our laboratory (figure 4), this tracked probe is used to localize three points on the specimen surface lying within the desired cutting plane, and three pins are inserted into these points to physically define this plane on the specimen. The specimen is then loaded into a ProCUT slotted forceps (Milestone Srl., Sorisole, Italy; Figure 3(b)), with the three pins placed within a single slot of the forceps, orienting the specimen for slicing along the desired plane. For stability during slicing, the specimen is supported using surrounding foam and steel lateral support plates inserted into adjacent slots in the forceps on either side of the prostate. After the apex is removed from the prostate, the prostate is placed within an agar block and processed as described above, yielding digital histopathology images taken every 5 mm throughout the gland.

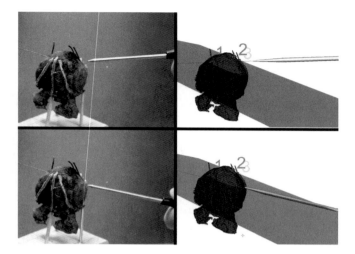

**Fig. 4.** Visualization software for image-guidance of gross specimen slicing. The visualization updates interactively to show the tracked probe interacting with the gland, giving visual feedback during fiducial and plane localization. Top row: the probe is out of the desired slicing plane, and the plane is shown in red for visual feedback that correction is necessary. Bottom row: the probe has been moved into the correct plane, which is now shown in green to indicate that the probe is correctly oriented to guide the insertion of a plane-marking pin.

It is important to note that although rigid registrations are used to map the desired *in vivo* slicing plane into the context of the *ex vivo* image and the specimen itself for pin-marking this plane, non-rigid registration (described in section 2.4) is used to determine the appropriate warp mapping the anatomy from the *in vivo* imaging context into the space of the digital histopathology images. The need for rigid registration in the procedure described above is driven by the fact that for practical reasons, the specimen must be sliced using a planar blade, and therefore there can be no out-of-plane deformation in the map from the *in vivo* image to the context of the specimen.

## 2.4   Image Registration

The transformations given by the registrations in figure 3 are then inverted in order to extract from the *in vivo* MR image the slice corresponding to each digital histopathology image. Next, an in-plane semi-automatic registration is performed using a thin-plate spline approach [13] in order to warp the *in vivo* MR image to match the digital histopathology image. To define the thin-plate spline, up to 20 anatomically corresponding landmark pairs are chosen in the images. The thin-plate spline then interpolates these correspondences to define a warp mapping the entire *in vivo* MR image plane into the space of the digital histopathology image.

## 3   Validation

In this work, we measure three sources of error in our procedure: (1) the accuracy with which the pins are inserted into the specimen, specifying the desired cutting plane; (2) the accuracy of making a cut along a plane specified by three pins using our modified ProCUT slotted forceps; and (3) the target registration error (TRE) of our thin-plate spline registration approach. We perform the first accuracy measurement by cutting a lamb kidney phantom such that it has two orthogonal flat sides (figure 5(a-b)). After inserting internal fiducial markers using the same procedure as for the prostates, we take a T1-weighted *ex vivo* MR image of this phantom using the identical protocol to that used during prostate specimen *ex vivo* imaging, with the coordinate system of the image oriented so that the flat sides are orthogonal to two of the image coordinate system axes. A desired cutting plane is determined in the space of the *ex vivo* image, parallel to the intersection line of the flat sides (dotted white segment in figure 5(a)), and the procedure described in section 2 is used to insert three pins within that plane. The phantom is then placed on a steel jig such that its flat sides are aligned to two of the axes of a milling machine, corresponding the 2D coordinate system given by the two yellow axes given in figure 5(a-b) in both the *ex vivo* image and the milling machine. A thin probe is inserted into the milling machine's chuck and its tip is used to localize the pin insertion points. The milling machine's digital readouts are used to provide 3D coordinates of pin insertion locations with 12.7 micron precision. The desired cutting plane is projected onto a line in the 2D coordinate system as shown in figure 5(a-b), and the pin insertion locations

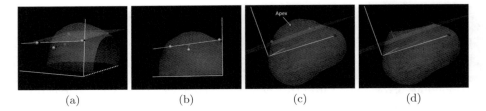

(a)          (b)          (c)          (d)

**Fig. 5.** (a-b) Measuring the accuracy of the insertion of pins within a desired specimen cutting plane. (a) A lamb kidney phantom cut to have two orthogonal flat sides (bottom and right). The yellow segments depict a 2D coordinate frame determined by vectors lying within, and orthogonal to the (dotted, white) intersection line of, the planes defined by the flat sides. The translucent plane in the figure indicates the desired plane of first cut. The green spheres indicate the insertion points of the three pins, intended to mark the cutting plane. (b) A rotated view of (a) showing the perpendicular distance measure used to determine pin insertion accuracy. (c-d) Measuring the accuracy of specimen slicing orientation. (c) The green spheres indicate insertion points of pins defining the desired cutting plane. The red spheres indicate the insertion points of three pins that are used to define an orthonormal frame of reference $F$ (yellow segments). (d) After the first cut, the insertion points indicated by the red spheres to determine $F$. The blue segment illustrates a single cutting accuracy measurement.

measured by the digital readouts are also projected onto that coordinate system. The disagreement between each measured pin and the desired cutting plane is measured in this 2D coordinate system as the Euclidean point-to-line distance as shown in figure 5(b).

We perform the second accuracy measurement on our prostate specimens, since cutting characteristics (e.g. tissue toughness, pliability) vary with tissue type. In addition to the three pins inserted to define the desired cutting plane (green spheres in figure 5(c)), we insert three additional pins (red spheres in figure 5(c-d) to define an orthonormal frame of reference for the desired cutting plane. The digital readouts on the milling machine are used to localize all pin insertion points, thus representing the desired cutting plane in terms of the coordinate system given by the yellow segments in figure 5(c-d). After the apex of the prostate is cut using the procedure given in section 2, the prostate is returned to the milling machine and the same coordinate system is reestablished by localizing the pin insertion points indicated by the red spheres (figure 5(d)). The digital readouts are then used to sample the 3D coordinates of eight equally-spaced points along the perimeter of the specimen cross section exposed by the cut, and the Euclidean distances between each of these points and the desired cutting plane is measured, as depicted in the blue segment on figure 5(d). These measurements indicate the amount by which the knife blade missed the desired cutting plane at the perimeter of the gland.

The third accuracy measurement is the post-registration TRE, which is a RMS error, of manually marked, corresponding fiducials in *in vivo* MR images and corresponding digital histology images. We perform a leave-one-out cross-validation experiment using the fiducial points that guide the TPS registration.

## 4    Results

Figure 6(a-b) qualitatively illustrates the anatomic concordance between a digital histopathology image and its corresponding registered *in vivo* MR image. The arrows in figure 6(a) are at the same locations in image space as the corresponding arrows in figure 6(b); note the alignment of the visible structures. Figure 6(c) shows the MR image before the in-plane warp, illustrating that much,

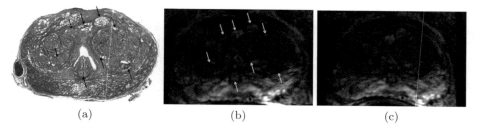

| (a) | (b) | (c) |

**Fig. 6.** A digital histopathology image (a) with corresponding registered MR image (b). (c) The MR image before application of the thin-plate spline warp.

but not all, of the deformation is due to pressure from the endorectal coil and inflated sheath during *in vivo* imaging. The results of the validation experiments (section 3) show a mean TRE of 0.85 mm (using 82 fiducials in 3 image pairs), a mean pin insertion error of 0.7 mm (2 trials, 6 pins total), and a mean slicing error of 0.6 mm (1 specimen, 8 sampled cross section points).

## 5 Conclusion

In this work, we have described and evaluated a method for registering *in vivo* prostate MR images to digital histopathology images. Our qualitative results demonstrate useful anatomic concordance resulting from the registration. In the first stage of our technique for orienting specimen slicing to improve image registration, pins defining the desired cutting plane are inserted into the specimen, and in the second stage, a specialized tool is used to slice along the plane defined by the pins. We have quantitatively validated our approach by measuring our TRE, as well as our accuracy at each of these two stages. Our TRE is 0.85 mm, and our mean errors in pin insertion and slicing are 0.7 mm and 0.6 mm, respectively, comparing favourably with our 2.2 mm diagnostic MR image thickness. Our registration results provide a proof of principle that useful registrations are achievable after orienting the slicing plane using our method. Ongoing research involves the use of our fiducial markers both to drive and evaluate non-rigid registration of the digital histopathology images to the *ex vivo* MR images, as well as non-rigid 3D registration of the *in vivo* and *ex vivo* MR images.

## References

1. Canadian Cancer Society's steering committee: Canadian Cancer Statistics 2009. Canadian Cancer Society, Toronto (2009)
2. Horner, M.J., Ries, L.A.G., Krapcho, M., Neyman, N., Aminou, R., Howlader, N., Altekruse, S.F., Feuer, E.J., Huang, L., Mariotto, A., Miller, B.A., Lewis, D.R., Eisner, M.P., Stinchcomb, D.G., Edwards, B.K. (eds.): SEER Cancer Statistics Review, 1975-2006. National Cancer Institute, Bethesda (2009), http://seer.cancer.gov/csr/1975_2006/
3. LaSpina, M., Haas, G.P.: Update on the diagnois and management of prostate cancer. Canadian Journal of Urology 15(suppl. 1), 3–13 (2008) (discussion 13)
4. Leite, K.R.M., Camara-Lopes, L.H.A., Dall'Oglio, M.F., Cury, J., Antunes, A.A., Sanudo, A., Srougi, M.: Upgrading the Gleason score in extended prostate biopsy: Implications for treatment choice. International Journal of Radiation Oncology Biology Physics 73, 353–356 (2009)
5. Ahmed, H.U., Kirkham, A., Arya, M., Illing, R., Freeman, A., Allen, C., Emberton, M.: Is it time to consider a role for MRI before prostate biopsy? Nature Reviews Clinical Oncology 6, 197–206 (2009)
6. Bax, J., Cool, D., Gardi, L., Knight, K., Smith, D., Montreuil, J., Sherebrin, S., Romagnoli, C., Fenster, A.: Mechanically assisted 3D ultrasound guided prostate biopsy system. Medical Physics 35(12), 5397–5410 (2008)

7. Cool, D., Sherebrin, S., Izawa, J., Chin, J., Fenster, A.: Design and evaluation of a 3D transrectal ultrasound prostate biopsy system. Medical Physics 35(10), 4695–4707 (2008)
8. Krieger, A., Susil, R.C., Ménard, C., Coleman, J.A., Fichtinger, G., Atalar, E., Whitcomb, L.L.: Design of a novel MRI compatible manipulator for image guided prostate interventions. IEEE Transactions on Biomedical Engineering 52(2), 306–313 (2005)
9. Polascik, T.J., Mouraviev, V.: Focal therapy for prostate cancer. Current Opinion in Urology 18(3), 269–274 (2008)
10. Rouvire, O., Reynolds, C., Hulshizer, T., Rossman, P., Le, Y., Felmlee, J.P., Ehman, R.L.: Mr histological correlation: A method for cutting specimens along the imaging plane in animal or ex vivo experiments. Journal of Magnetic Resonance Imaging 23, 60–69 (2006)
11. Shah, V., Pohida, T., Turkbey, B., Mani, H., Merino, M., Pinto, P., Choykey, P., Bernardo, M.: A method for correlating in vivo prostate magnetic resonance imaging and histopathology using individualized magnetic resonance-based molds. Review of Scientific Instruments 80, 104301 (2009)
12. Ourselin, S., Roche, A., Prima, A., Ayache, N.: Block matching: A general framework to improve robustness of rigid registration of medical images. In: Niessen, W.J., Viergever, M.A. (eds.) MICCAI 2001. LNCS, vol. 2208, pp. 557–566. Springer, Heidelberg (2001)
13. Bookstein, F.L.: Principal warps: Thin-plate splines and the decomposition of deformations. IEEE Transactions on Pattern Analysis and Machine Intelligence 11(6), 567–585 (1989)

# High-Throughput Prostate Cancer Gland Detection, Segmentation, and Classification from Digitized Needle Core Biopsies

Jun Xu[1], Rachel Sparks[1], Andrew Janowcyzk[1,3], John E. Tomaszewski[2],
Michael D. Feldman[2], and Anant Madabhushi[1]

[1] Department of Biomedical Engineering, Rutgers University, USA
[2] The Hospital of the University of Pennsylvania, Anatomic and Surgical Pathology
Informatics, Philadelphia, USA
[3] Department of Computer Science and Engineering, Indian Institute of Technology
(IIT) Bombay, Mumbai, India

**Abstract.** We present a high-throughput computer-aided system for the segmentation and classification of glands in high resolution digitized images of needle core biopsy samples of the prostate. It will allow for rapid and accurate identification of suspicious regions on these samples. The system includes the following three modules: 1) a hierarchical frequency weighted mean shift normalized cut (HNCut) for initial detection of glands; 2) a geodesic active contour (GAC) model for gland segmentation; and 3) a diffeomorphic based similarity (DBS) feature extraction for classification of glands as benign or cancerous. HNCut is a minimally supervised color based detection scheme that combines the frequency weighted mean shift and normalized cuts algorithms to detect the lumen region of candidate glands. A GAC model, initialized using the results of HNCut, uses a color gradient based edge detection function for accurate gland segmentation. Lastly, DBS features are a set of morphometric features derived from the nonlinear dimensionality reduction of a dissimilarity metric between shape models. The system integrates these modules to enable the rapid detection, segmentation, and classification of glands on prostate biopsy images. Across 23 H & E stained prostate studies of whole-slides, 105 regions of interests (ROIs) were selected for the evaluation of segmentation and classification. The segmentation results were evaluated on 10 ROIs and compared to manual segmentation in terms of mean distance ($2.6 \pm 0.2$ pixels), overlap ($62 \pm 0.07\%$), sensitivity ($85 \pm 0.01\%$), specificity ($94 \pm 0.003\%$) and positive predictive value ($68 \pm 0.08\%$). Over 105 ROIs, the classification accuracy for glands automatically segmented was ($82.5 \pm 9.10\%$) while the accuracy for glands manually segmented was ($82.89 \pm 3.97\%$); no statistically significant differences were identified between the classification results.

**Keywords:** High-throughput, geodesic active contour model, morphological feature, prostate cancer, glands, needle biopsy, digital pathology.

A. Madabhushi et al. (Eds.): Prostate Cancer Imaging 2010, LNCS 6367, pp. 77–88, 2010.
© Springer-Verlag Berlin Heidelberg 2010

# 1   Introduction

Digital pathology is a rapidly expanding field for the analysis, viewing, and storage of histology tissue samples due to the advent and cost-effectiveness of whole-slide digital scanners [1]. In the context of prostate cancer (CaP), pathologists grade histopathological specimens by visually characterizing gland morphology and architecture in regions they suspect are malignant. The Gleason grading system is used to describe CaP aggressiveness; nonaggressive glands (grade 1) are medium-sized with round shapes, while aggressive glands (grade 5) are small and have irregular shapes [2]. CaP grading of histopathology can therefore be divided into two separate tasks: identification of malignant regions and the Gleason grading of the malignant regions. The ability to quickly and accurately identify suspicious regions in tissue samples will enable the pathologist to focus their grading efforts on candidate regions, minimizing the time spent on identifying CaP regions. Doyle *et al.* [3] have demonstrated the effectiveness for discriminating malignant regions using texture based features at low image resolutions. Recently, Monaco *et al.* [4] showed that gland size can be used to discriminate between malignant and benign glands on high resolution whole mount histopathology of the prostate. Automated schemes for Gleason grading of suspicious regions on prostate histopathology have attempted to leverage gland morphology by quantifying contour variability, length-to-width ratio, or related features [5], [6]. We have recently demonstrated that Diffeomorphic Based Similarity (DBS) features are better able to capture subtle morphometric differences between prostate glands of different Gleason grades than previously reported morphological features [7].

An important pre-requisite to extracting morphological features is the ability to accurately and efficiently detect the location of glands and segment them accurately while preserving important morphological information. While active contour models are good candidate for this task, most active contour models are not able to efficiently handle very large images. Region-based active contour models do not require accurate contour initialization, however they may involve significant computational overhead [8]. Hence, there is a need for rapid identification of the regions of interest in order to initialize the active contour model. Hierarchical mean shift normalized cuts (HNCut) was shown to efficiently determine the location of the region of interest on very large histopathology images [9]. Additionally, for most boundary based active contour models, the evolution function is dependent on the gray scale intensity gradient [10]. We employ a local structure tensor based color gradient, obtained by calculating the local min/max variations contributed from each color channel (e.g. R, G, B or H, S, V), resulting in stronger object boundaries compared to the gray scale gradient.

We present a system which applies a geodesic active contour (GAC) model in conjunction with DBS feature extraction to effectively segment and classify the glandular regions of needle core biopsies of the prostate in a high-throughput manner. Figure 1 shows the flowchart of our system which is comprised of three modules. Module 1 identifies glands using HNCut, an accurate, efficient, and minimally interactive model initialization scheme HNCut. In module 2, our GAC model initialized by HNCut finds the gland boundaries utilizing a color gradient based edge-detector function. In module 3, DBS features are obtained by computing differences between medial axis shape models of glands, followed by nonlinear dimensionality reduction (Graph Embedding [11]) to extract relevant morphometric features. DBS features are used to train a SVM classifier for distinguishing between malignant and benign glands.

Our high-throughput system requires minimal human interaction. HNCut only requires a few reference colors selected from a region of interest on a single representative image. Our system is then able to automatically segment and classify the target objects on the remaining images in the dataset without the need for further human interaction. While in this work our system is evaluated in the context of segmentation and classification of glands on prostate histopathology images, the system could be applied to a wide domain of problems where precise quantification of morphological traits is critical, such as breast lesion morphology on DCE-MRI [12].

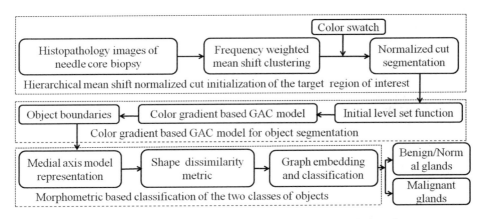

**Fig. 1.** Flowchart of our integrated detection, segmentation, and classification system

## 2   Gland Detection and Segmentation

### 2.1   Notation

The following notations will be used throughout the paper: $\mathcal{C} = (C, f)$ denotes the 2D image scene where $C \in \mathbb{R}^2$ is a grid of pixels $c \in C$. The pixels $c$ are in a 2D Cartesian grid defined by $c = (x, y)$. The image intensity function $\mathbf{f}(c)$ assigns a three element intensity vector to pixel $c \in C$. The level set function is defined as $\phi(t, c)$. $\mathbb{C} = \{c \in \Omega : \phi(c) = 0\}$ is the zero level set. $\Omega$ denotes a bounded open set in $\mathbb{R}^2$ space. $\Omega_f = \{c \in \Omega : \phi(c) > 0\}$ denotes a foreground region while $\Omega_b = \{c \in \Omega : \phi(c) < 0\}$ denotes the background region. $\| \cdot \|$ denotes the $L_2$ normal in real space. $\delta(\phi)$ is the Delta function.

## 2.2   Hierarchical Mean Shift Based Normalized Cuts Detection Scheme

The hierarchical mean shift based normalized cuts (HNCut) scheme was originally presented in [9] for rapidly and accurately segmenting the object class of
interest. By operating in the color domain, as opposed to the spatial domain
(on pixels), the scheme is able to rapidly identify the gland regions even on very
large images. The scheme is outlined below:

1. User selects the domain swatch defined as a set of pixels that are representative of the target class;
2. Frequency weighted mean-shift clustering is performed on a multi-resolution
   color pyramid;
3. Normalized cuts is used on the reduced color space created by the weighted
   mean-shift algorithm.

HNCut is robust to human intervention; the first step is only applied to a single
representative image containing the target class. After the color swatch has been
selected from the region of interest in the first image, the same swatch may be
applied to all other images. The resulting target objects make for an excellent
initialization of the active contour model that is subsequently applied.

## 2.3   Geodesic Active Contour Model

**Energy functional.** Assume the image plane $\Omega \in \mathbb{R}^2$ is partitioned into 2
non-overlapping regions by a zero level set function $\phi$: the foreground $\Omega_f$ and
background $\Omega_b$. The optimal partition of the image plane $\Omega$ by a zero level set
function $\phi$ can be obtained through minimizing the energy functional as follows,

$$E(\phi) = \alpha E_1(\phi) + \beta E_2(\phi) + \gamma E_3(\phi), \tag{1}$$

$$= \alpha \int_C g(\mathbf{f}(c))dc + \beta \int_{\Omega_f} g(\mathbf{f}(c))dc + \gamma \int_\Omega \frac{1}{2}(\|\nabla\phi\| - 1)^2 dc,$$

where $E_1(\phi)$ is the energy functional of a traditional GAC model. $E_2(\phi)$ is in-
spired by the balloon force proposed in [13]. An additional term $E_3(\phi)$ is added
to the energy functional to remove the re-initialization phase which is required
as a numerical remedy for maintaining stable curve evolution in traditional level
set methods [14].

**The color gradient.** The edge-detector function in the traditional GAC model
and the balloon force are based on the calculation of the gray scale gradient of
the image [10]. In this paper, the edge-detector function is based on the color
gradient which is defined as $g(\mathbf{f}(c)) = \frac{1}{1+s(\mathbf{f}(c))}$. $s(\mathbf{f}(c))$ is the local structure tensor based color gradient which is defined as $s(\mathbf{f}(c)) = \sqrt{\lambda_+ - \lambda_-}$ [15], where $\lambda_+$
and $\lambda_-$ are the maximum and minimum eigenvalues of the local structure tensor
of each pixel in the image. It locally sums the gradient contributions from each
image channel representing the extreme rates of change in the direction of their
corresponding eigenvectors. The methodology for computing the color gradient

described above can be applied to different vectorial color representations such as RGB, HSV, and Luv.

**Curve evolution function of GAC model.** Based on the theory of the calculus of variations, the curve evolution function can be derived from the level set framework by minimizing the energy functional (1). The function is defined by the following partial differential equation:

$$\begin{cases} \frac{\partial \phi}{\partial t} = \delta(\phi)\{\alpha \mathbf{div}\left[g(\mathbf{f}(c))\frac{\nabla \phi}{\|\nabla \phi\|}\right] - \beta g(\mathbf{f}(c))\} - \gamma \left[\Delta \phi - \mathbf{div}(\frac{\nabla \phi}{\|\nabla \phi\|})\right], \\ \phi(0, c) = \phi_0(c), \end{cases} \quad (2)$$

where $\alpha$, $\beta$, and $\gamma$ are positive constant parameters, and $\phi_0(c)$ is the initial evolution functional which is obtained from the HNCut detection results (see Section 2.2). $\mathbf{div}(\cdot)$ is the divergence operator. As the re-initialization phase has been removed, $\phi_0$ is defined as piecewise linear function of regions:

$$\phi_0(c) = \begin{cases} -\pi, & c \in \Omega_b; \\ 0, & c \in \mathbb{C}; \\ \pi, & c \in \Omega_f, \end{cases}$$

where $\Omega_f$, $\mathbb{C}$, and $\Omega_b$ in the context of the problem addressed in this paper are the luminal regions, the boundaries of the luminal regions and the other tissues, respectively. $\pi$ is a positive constant.

## 3  Diffeomorphic Based Shape Characterization and Classification

### 3.1  Medial Axis Shape Model

The medial axis shape model $M$ is defined by a set of pixels $m \in \Omega_f$ along the medial axis of an object, and a set of corresponding surface vectors $\boldsymbol{v}_1$, $\boldsymbol{v}_2$ on the contour $\mathbb{C}$. Here $\boldsymbol{v}_1$, $\boldsymbol{v}_2$ are comprised by the nearest pixels on the contour $\mathbb{C}$ to the medial axis pixel $m$ [16]. For a given object, we can define a distance map function $f^e(c)$ on the image space as, $f^e(c) = \begin{cases} 0 & c \in \mathbb{C}, \\ -\min_{p\in\mathbb{C}} \|c - p\| & c \in \Omega_f, \\ \min_{p\in\mathbb{C}} \|c - p\| & c \in \Omega_b. \end{cases}$

Given this distance map, the medial axis is the local minimum along the gradient map of the image, defined as $\widehat{f}^e(c) = \left(\frac{\partial f^e(c)}{\partial x}\right)^2 + \left(\frac{\partial f^e(c)}{\partial y}\right)^2$. Atoms belonging to the medial axis are obtained as $M = \{m : m \in C, \widehat{f}^e(m) < \tau\}$. Empirically, $\{\tau = 0.05 \left[\min_{c\in C}(\widehat{f}(c)^e)\right]\}$ was found to give a well defined medial axis. $\forall m \in M$, the two closest pixels on the contour $\mathbb{C}$ can be defined as $\widehat{p}_1 = \underset{p\in\mathbb{C}}{\operatorname{argmin}}\|m - p\|$,

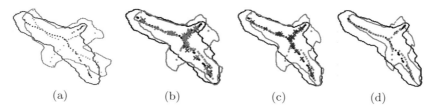

|     |     |     |     |
| --- | --- | --- | --- |
| (a) | (b) | (c) | (d) |

**Fig. 2.** (a) Two gland contours (black $\mathbb{C}_a$, gray $\mathbb{C}_b$) with corresponding medial atoms (blue $M_a$, green $M_b$) after initial affine alignment. Medial atoms for the fifth iteration with cluster centers of the shape models (light blue, dark green) for (b) initial cluster centers and (c) registration of cluster centers. Note cluster centers are aligned between the two gland contours after the registration. (d) The medial atoms of gland contours after final registration

and $\widehat{p}_2 = \underset{p \in \mathbb{C}, p \neq \widehat{p}_1}{\mathrm{argmin}} \|m - p\|$, and the corresponding surface vectors are defined $\boldsymbol{v}_1 = \widehat{p}_1 - m$, and $\boldsymbol{v}_2 = \widehat{p}_2 - m$.

## 3.2   Medial Axis Model Comparison

A dissimilarity metric is calculated between each pair of medial axis representations $M_i$ and $M_j$, where $i, j \in \{1, \ldots, N\}$. Here $N$ refers to the number of glands. Briefly the steps of the comparison are:

1. $M_i$ is registered to $M_j$ using a point-based diffeomorphic registration algorithm originally presented in [17]. Fuzzy $k$-means clustering determines correspondences between the medial axis models. From these correspondences, a diffeomorphic transformation is calculated to register $M_i$ into the coordinate space of $M_j$. This process is iteratively repeated until a stopping criteria is met. Figure 2 shows an example of this registration technique displaying the initial alignment, a single clustering and registration step, and the final alignment.
2. Point correspondence between the medial atom sets $\tilde{m}_i^{\widehat{u}} \in \tilde{M}_i$ and $m_j^{\widehat{v}} \in M_j$ is found. We define $\tilde{M}_i$ as the medial axis $M_i$ registered to the medial axis model $M_j$. We determine point correspondence between two medial axes as,$(\widehat{u}, \widehat{v}) = \underset{\widehat{u}, \widehat{v}}{\mathrm{argmin}} \|\tilde{m}_i^u - m_j^v\|$.
3. From the point correspondences in Step 2, shape dissimilarity is calculated as

$$A_{ij} = \sum_{(\widehat{u}, \widehat{v})} \kappa_1 \|m_i^{\widehat{u}} - m_j^{\widehat{v}}\| + \kappa_2 \|\boldsymbol{v}_{i,1}^{\widehat{u}} - \boldsymbol{v}_{j,1}^{\widehat{v}}\| + \kappa_3 \|\boldsymbol{v}_{i,2}^{\widehat{u}} - \boldsymbol{v}_{j,2}^{\widehat{v}}\|. \quad (3)$$

where $\kappa_1$, $\kappa_2$, and $\kappa_3 > 0$ are selected so that $A_{ab} \geq 0$.

The medial axis model comparison is repeated over all objects $i, j \in \{1, \ldots, N\}$, so that $A \in \mathbb{R}^{N \times N}$ is a high dimensional dissimilarity matrix.

### 3.3    Feature Extraction

From $A$, we define similarity matrix $W$, where $W_{ij} = e^{-A_{ij}/\sigma}$, and $\sigma > 0$ controls the width of the neighborhoods. $D$ is diagonal matrix whose diagonal elements are defined as $d_{ii} = \sum_j W_{ij}$. Here $A_{ij}$ and $W_{ij}$ are elements of matrices $A$ and $W$, respectively. From the Laplacian matrix $D - W$, we find a low dimensional space $\mathbf{Y} = (\mathbf{y}^{(1)}, \mathbf{y}^{(2)}, \ldots, \mathbf{y}^{(N)})^T \in \mathbb{R}^{N \times d}$, where $N >> d$, that attempts to preserve pairwise distances between glands in $A$. Let $\mathbf{Y}^*$ be the set of all $N \times d$ matrices $\mathbf{Y}$ such that $\mathbf{Y}^T D \mathbf{Y} = \mathbf{I}_d$. The DBS features of each gland will be determined from the optimal $\mathbf{Y} \in \mathbf{Y}^*$ by solving the following minimization problem [11]

$$\min_{\mathbf{Y} \in \mathbf{Y}^*} \sum_{i=1}^{N} \sum_{j=1}^{N} \|\mathbf{y}^{(i)} - \mathbf{y}^{(j)}\|^2 W_{ij} = tr(\mathbf{Y^T}(D - W)\mathbf{Y}), \qquad (4)$$

$$s.t \qquad\qquad \mathbf{Y^T} D \mathbf{Y} = \mathbf{I}_d$$

where $\mathbf{y}^{(i)} = (y_1(i), y_2(i), \ldots, y_d(i))^{\mathbf{T}}$ is the $d$-dimensional representation of the $i$-th gland and $\mathbf{I}_d$ is the $d$-dimensional identity matrix. Each row vector in $\mathbf{Y}$ is used to determine $d$-dimensional DBS features of a corresponding gland, where $d = 3$ in this work.

## 4    Experimental Design and Performance Measures

### 4.1    Data Description

The data set includes digitized images of whole-slide prostate needle core biopsy specimens obtained from 23 patients and stained with Hematoxylin & Eosin (H&E). All studies were obtained from the Hospital at the University of Pennsylvania (UPENN). Each sample was digitized at 20x optical magnification using an Aperio whole-slide digital scanner. For all images, an expert pathologist manually annotated regions of interest (ROI) with different class labels: benign epithelium, benign stroma, and Gleason grades 3 and 4. Within each ROI, a human observer manually segmented the lumen layer of each gland. A total of 105 ROIs were identified consisting of benign (23 ROIs, 66 glands), Gleason grade 3 (71 ROIs, 656 glands), and grade 4 (11 ROIs, 36 glands).

### 4.2    Quantitative Evaluation of Segmentation

Owing to the great deal of manual labor involved in segmenting the gland boundaries, we limited the quantitative evaluation to only glands present within 10 ROIs from 10 whole-slide images randomly selected. The boundaries of automated segmentation are defined as the contours of the zero level set function of active contour models after convergence. We evaluate the segmentation results via two types of measurements. For boundary-based measurements, mean absolute distance (MAD) was calculated as $\mathrm{MAD} = \frac{1}{s} \sum_{\nu=1}^{s} \{\min_{\chi} \|c_\nu - c_\chi\|\}, \quad \forall c_\chi \in \mathcal{G}, \quad \forall c_\nu \in \mathcal{S}$

where $\mathcal{G} = \{c_\chi | \chi \in \{1, \ldots, t\}\}$ and $\mathcal{S} = \{c_\nu | \nu \in \{1, \ldots, s\}\}$ are closed boundaries of manual and automated segmentation, respectively. $t$ and $s$ represent the number of pixels on the boundaries of manual and automated segmentation, respectively. For region-based measurements we calculated overlap (OL), sensitivity (SN), specificity (SP), and positive predictive value (PPV). For each image, the set of pixels lying within the manual delineations of the glands is denoted as $\mathcal{A}(G)$. $\mathcal{A}(S)$ is the set of pixels whose level set functions are positive, after the convergence of active contour model. OL, SN, SP, and PPV are then defined as OL $= \frac{|\mathcal{A}(S) \cap \mathcal{A}(G)|}{|\mathcal{A}(S) \cup \mathcal{A}(G)|}$, SN $= \frac{|\mathcal{A}(S) \cap \mathcal{A}(G)|}{|\mathcal{A}(G)|}$, SP $= \frac{|C - \mathcal{A}(S) \cup \mathcal{A}(G)|}{|C - \mathcal{A}(G)|}$, and PPV $= \frac{|\mathcal{A}(S) \cap \mathcal{A}(G)|}{|\mathcal{A}(S)|}$, where $|\mathcal{S}|$ represents the cardinality of set $\mathcal{S}$.

### 4.3  Morphological Feature Set Evaluation

A support vector machine (SVM) classifier [18] was used to evaluate the discriminability of the DBS features, with higher SVM accuracy reflecting a feature set that is better able to describe morphometric differences between gland classes. In this experiment we (a) compare the performance of the DBS features versus traditional boundary based attributes (area, perimeter, area overlap ratio, average radial distance ratio, standard deviation of the normalized distance ratio, compactness, and smoothness [12]) and (b) evaluate whether, from a gland classification perspective, the results obtained from automated and manual segmentation were significantly different. Four feature sets were tested comprising of DBS or traditional morphological features from either automated or manual gland segmentations.

For all feature sets malignant glands were defined as all glands contained within ROIs of a Gleason grade 3 or 4, while benign glands are obtained from benign ROIs. The SVM classifier accuracy was evaluated by utilizing a leave-one-study-out approach. The leave-one-study-out approach selected a testing set consisting of all glands from one patient study while the training set was comprised of glands from the remaining 22 patient studies. We evaluated the accuracy of our automated segmentation by performing a paired t-test over all 23 test sets between automated and manual segmentation for each feature set. We hypothesize that if no significant difference is found between the classification accuracies of the manual and automated schemes, the automated segmentation results are as good as the manual segmentation.

## 5  Experimental Results and Discussion

### 5.1  Segmentation Evaluation

Table 1 shows the results of quantitative evaluation of segmentation by our automated GAC scheme in terms of MAD, OL, SN, SP and PPV across 10 ROIs from

**Table 1.** Quantitative evaluation of segmentation results for the system. The average and standard deviation of the MAD, OL, SN, SP and PPV over 40 glands and 10 ROI's have been reported

| MAD | Overlap (OL) | Sensitivity ($SN$) | Specificity ($SP$) | PPV |
|---|---|---|---|---|
| $2.06 \pm 0.2$ | $0.62 \pm 0.07$ | $0.85 \pm 0.01$ | $0.94 \pm 0.003$ | $0.68 \pm 0.08$ |

**Table 2.** SVM classification accuracy evaluated for manual and automated segmentation as well as DBS or common morphological features sets for a leave-one-patient-out evaluation. Accuracy was calculated for 23 different testing sets. The $p$-values reported test the hypothesis that the underlying distributions are statistically dissimilar. In both cases the null hypothesis, the distribution are statistically similar, was accepted

| Morphological Feature | Segmentation | Accuracy- Annotated Regions | P-Value |
|---|---|---|---|
| Common | Manual | $79.47 \pm 4.71\%$ | 0.989 |
| | Automated | $81.30 \pm 10.14\%$ | |
| DBS | Manual | **$82.89 \pm 3.97\%$** | 0.9596 |
| | Automated | $82.50 \pm 9.10\%$ | |

10 patient studies. The mean and standard deviation values in Table 1 show that our HNCut based GAC scheme is able to segment the lumen regions accurately.

## 5.2 DBS Feature Evaluation

Table 2 shows that for both morphological feature types, the source of the gland boundaries (manual or automated) did not affect the SVM's ability to classify glands. For both features sets, $p$-values are not statistically significant ($p < 0.05$), so we accept the null hypothesis that the classifier accuracy using features derived from the manual and automated segmentation are similar. DBS yields higher classifier accuracy compared to traditional morphological features, although this difference is not statistically significant.

Qualitative results are illustrated in Figure 3 (a). Three regions have been shown in Figures 3 (b), (c) and (d), respectively. From the magnified regions, one can see that the lumen regions have been correctly segmented. The corresponding explicit medial axis shape models of segmented glands, consisting of pixels belonging to the medial axis (light blue) and surface vectors (dark blue), are shown in Figures 3 (e), (f) and (g), respectively. Figure 4 illustrates the classification results obtained from module 3. In Figure 4(a), the region annotated by the blue line is the malignant portion of the slide as determined by the expert pathologist. Gland boundaries are displayed for glands labeled benign (black) and malignant (green). From Figure 4(a), we can see that most of the segmented glands are correctly classified, with most of the errors occurring at the borders.

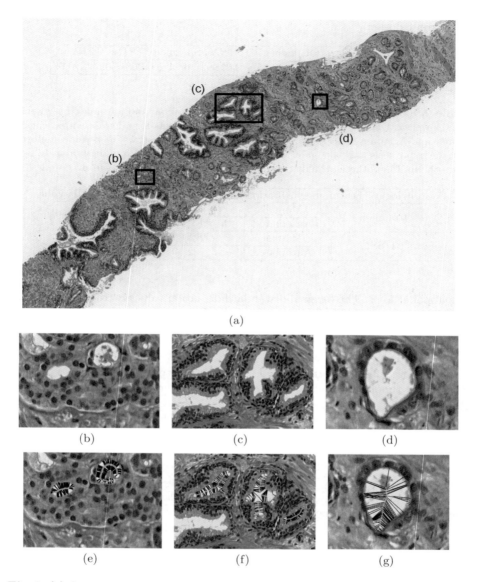

**Fig. 3.** (a) A representative example of the gland segmentation results (boundaries in green) from a whole-slide needle core biopsy. (b), (c), and (d) are three different ROIs from (a) which have been magnified to show gland details. The corresponding explicit medial axis shape model, consisting of the medial axis (light blue) and surface vectors (dark blue) are shown in (e), (f) and (g), respectively

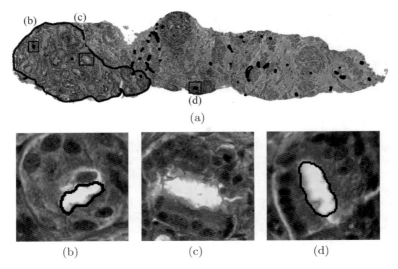

**Fig. 4.** (a) An example of whole-slide needle core biopsy of the prostate with malignant region delineated in blue. Glands labeled as benign/normal (black) and malignant (green) by the DBS SVM classifier are displayed. (b) An example of a malignant gland mislabeled by the DBS base classifier as benign. (c) A correctly labeled malignant and (d) benign gland by the DBS SVM classifier

## 6 Concluding Remarks

In this paper, we presented a high-throughput system for rapid and accurate gland detection, segmentation, and classification on high resolution digitized images of needle core biopsy samples of the prostate. The system is comprised of three modules: 1) a hierarchical mean shift normalized cut (HNCut) for initial gland detection, 2) a color gradient based geodesic active contour (GAC) model initialized via the result of HNCut, and the use of 3) a diffeomorphic based similarity (DBS) features to classify glands as benign or cancerous. The system requires minimal human interaction. The effectiveness of the automated segmentation of glands and the DBS features to distinguish cancerous and benign glands were evaluated and compared against corresponding manual segmentation obtained from 23 H & E stained prostate studies. Classification accuracy in distinguishing benign from malignant glands when using the automated segmentation scheme was $82.5 \pm 9.10\%$, while the corresponding accuracy with manual segmentation was $82.89 \pm 3.97\%$; no statistically significant differences were identified between the two segmentation schemes.

## References

1. Madabhushi, A.: Digital pathology image analysis: opportunities and challenges. Imaging in Medicine 1(1), 7–10 (2009)
2. Gleason, D.F.: Histologic grading of prostate cancer: A perspective. Human Pathology 23(3), 273–279 (1992); The Pathobiology of Prostate Cancer-Part 1

3. Doyle, S., Feldman, M., Tomaszewski, J., Madabhushi, A.: A boosted bayesian multi-resolution classifier for prostate cancer detection from digitized needle biopsies. IEEE Transactions on Biomedical Engineering (in Press)
4. Monaco, J.P., Tomaszewski, J.E., Feldman, M.D., Hagemann, I., Moradi, M., Mousavi, P., Boag, A., Davidson, C., Abolmaesumi, P., Madabhushi, A.: High-throughput detection of prostate cancer in histological sections using probabilistic pairwise markov models. Medical Image Analysis 14, 617–629 (2010)
5. Farjam, R., Soltanian-Zadeh, H., Jafari-Khouzani, K., Zoroofi, R.: An image analysis approach for automatic malignancy determination of prostate pathological images. Cytometry Part B (Clinical Cytometry) 72(B), 227–240 (2007)
6. Tabesh, A., Teverovskiy, M., Ho-Yuen, P., Kumar, V.P., Verbel, D., Kotsianti, A., Saidi, O.: Multifeature prostate cancer diagnosis and gleason grading of histological images. IEEE Transactions on Medical Imaging 26(10), 1366–1378 (2007)
7. Sparks, R., Madabhushi, A.: Novel morphometric based classification via diffeomorphic based shape representation using manifold learning. In: MICCAI 2010 (2010) (in press)
8. Paragios, N., Deriche, R.: Geodesic active regions and level set methods for supervised texture segmentation. International Journal of Computer Vision 46(3), 223–247 (2002)
9. Janowczyk, A., Chandran, S., Singh, R., Sasaroli, D., Coukos, G., Feldman, M.D., Madabhushi, A.: Hierarchical normalized cuts: Unsupervised segmentation of vascular biomarkers from ovarian cancer tissue microarrays. In: Yang, G.-Z., Hawkes, D., Rueckert, D., Noble, A., Taylor, C. (eds.) MICCAI 2009. LNCS, vol. 5761, pp. 230–238. Springer, Heidelberg (2009)
10. Caselles, V., Kimmel, R., Sapiro, G.: Geodesic active contours. International Journal of Computer Vision 22(1), 61–79 (1997)
11. Belkin, M., Niyogi, P.: Laplacian eigenmaps for dimensionality reduction and data representation. Neural Computation 15(6), 1373–1396 (2003)
12. Agner, S., Soman, S., Libfeld, E., McDonald, M., Thomas, K., Englander, S., Rosen, M., Chin, D., Nosher, J., Madabhushi, A.: Textural kinetics: A novel dynamic contrast enhanced (DCE)- MRI feature for breast lesion classification. Journal of Digital Imaging (in press)
13. Cohen, L.D.: On active contour models and balloons. CVGIP: Image Underst. 53(2), 211–218 (1991)
14. Li, C., Xu, C., Gui, C., Fox, M.D.: Level set evolution without re-initialization: A new variational formulation. In: CVPR, vol. 1, pp. 430–436 (2005)
15. Sapiro, G.: Color snakes. Computer Vision and Image Understanding 68(2), 247–253 (1997)
16. Blum, H.: A transformation for extracting new descriptors of shape. In: Models for the Perception of Speech and Visual Form, pp. 367–380. MIT Press, Cambridge (1967)
17. Guo, H., Rangarajan, A., Joshi, S.: Diffeomorphic point matching. In: Handbook of Mathematical Models in Computer Vision, pp. 205–219. Springer, US (2005)
18. Cortes, C., Vapnik, V.: Support-vector networks. Machine Learning 20, 273–297 (1995)

# Automated Analysis of PIN-4 Stained Prostate Needle Biopsies

Bikash Sabata, Boris Babenko, Robert Monroe, and Chukka Srinivas

BioImagene Inc., 919 Hermosa Court, Sunnyvale, CA 94085
Bikash.Sabata@bioimagene.com
http://www.bioimagene.com

**Abstract.** Prostate Needle biopsies are stained with the PIN-4 marker cocktail to help the pathologist distinguish between HGPIN and adenocarcinoma. The correct interpretation of multiple IHC markers can be challenging. Therefore we propose the use of computer aided diagnosis algorithms for the identification and classification of glands in a whole slide image of prostate needle biopsy. The paper presents the different issues related to the automated analysis of prostate needle biopsies and the approach taken by BioImagene in its first generation algorithms.

**Keywords:** Computer Aided Diagnostics (CAD), Prostate Analysis, Medical Imaging, Histopathology Image Analysis.

## 1 Introduction

Several immunohistochemistry (IHC) markers are routinely used by pathologists in the interpretation of prostate biopsies, including P504S (racemace), p63, and high molecular weight (HMW) cytokeratins (CK5 and CK14) [1]. P504S is a protein preferentially expressed in the cytoplasm of prostatic adenocarcinoma as well as high-grade prostatic intraepithelial neoplasia (HGPIN). p63 and the HMW cytokeratins are expressed in the nucleus and cytoplasm respectively of prostatic basal cells surrounding benign prostatic glands, but not in the secretory cells of these glands [2]. The combination of these markers in the PIN-4 antibody cocktail (Biocare) is useful to the pathologist in the distinction between adenocarcinoma, HGPIN, and benign glands, particularly in cases with limited tissue [3]. However, correct interpretation of multiple IHC markers staining different subcellular compartments of different cell types can be challenging. Computer aided image analysis (CAD) algorithms are therefore required to assist the pathologist in the interpretation of prostatic tissue stained with the PIN-4 cocktail.

The workflow within the clinical labs is optimized to maximize the number of cases a pathologist can sign out without compromising the quality of diagnosis. Digital pathology promises to create the transformation to pathology practice that increases the overall quality and quantity of pathology diagnosis. The pathology slides are scanned using the whole slide scanner such as the iScan device from BioImagene. The images generated are managed within a workflow

A. Madabhushi et al. (Eds.): Prostate Cancer Imaging 2010, LNCS 6367, pp. 89–100, 2010.
© Springer-Verlag Berlin Heidelberg 2010

software such as Virtuoso. The pathologist reviews the slides and selects regions in the images for analysis. The CAD algorithms for interpretation of PIN-4 marker cocktail in prostate glands consist of two steps. In the first step we detect and identify the glands within the needle biopsy and in the second step we classify each of the detected glands.

The paper describes the challenges associated with the segmentation, identification and classification of prostate glands in PIN-4 stained needle biopsies. We also present some experiments conducted to compare the CAD classification with the manual classification on whole slide images.

## 2    Approach

Whole slide images generated for Digital Pathology are typically Gigapixel images that require a scalable computational infrastructure to support the data volume. We have developed a pathology image analysis platform called *iAnalytics* that is able to handle such data volumes. In addition, the *iAnalytics* framework has a layered component based architecture that allows for the rapid development of scalable algorithms for pathology CAD. The system is developed in C++ and has interfaces to other languages such as Java, C#, Python and Matlab.

The components in *iAnalytics* are arranged in 3 layers (figure 1). At the bottom layer, interfaces to external low level imaging libraries are maintained through wrappers that allow these libraries to be plugged in or replaced. We have specifically integrated with the Intel IPP, Intel MKL, FreeImage [4] and OpenCV [5] libraries. The Imaging layer above this consists of the basic classes

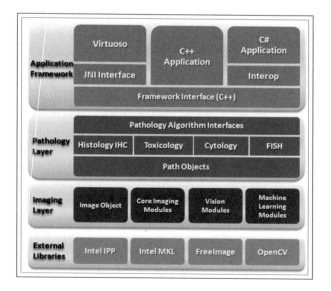

**Fig. 1.** iAnalytics Component Based Layered Architecture

needed for creating imaging objects and processing them. Image processing functions that are available in the off-the shelf commercial and open source systems are used with wrapper classes. In addition, we have implemented a large collection of basic imaging modules that include color processing, texture processing, and morphological operations. Vision modules that compute different types of features are also implemented in this layer. Most of the vision modules are high performance implementations of well known algorithms. Proprietary techniques have also been developed and included in the framework for the pathology domain that specialize well known techniques to the domain. Finally, classes implementing different types of Machine Learning techniques are included in the Imaging layer. The topmost layer of iAnalytics implements the components associated with the pathology CAD algorithms. High level pathology objects such as cells, nuclei, membrane, tissue regions, and glands are implemented as compositions of the lower layer objects. The pathology objects are combined together to define a CAD algorithm. All algorithms are accessed through a common interface. New algorithms that are developed can easily be included within existing applications that implement the interface framework. The *iAnalytics* component architecture allows the development of new algorithms as a composition of existing components.

## 2.1   Workflows

The automated analysis of PIN-4 stained prostate needle biopsies is supported within two different types of workflows. In the first workflow, the pathologist follows the steps enumerated below:

1. Select the case to be reviewed
2. Select the PIN-4 slide within the case to be reviewed
3. Review the virtual whole slide image at different resolutions and identify potential regions of tumor
4. Select the region encompassing the tumor using the FOV (Field of View) selection tool
5. Invoke the analysis algorithm on the FOV
6. The analysis algorithm automatically segments and identifies the individual glands within the FOV
7. The algorithm then classifies the individual glands
8. Finally, the algorithm in addition to the gland class, reports on some of the measurements on the gland (tumor area, median intensity).

In the above workflow the identification of the region is carried out by the pathologist. The onus of identifying all regions with tumor and carrying out the analysis is left to the pathologist. The second workflow is more complex but makes the job of the pathologist easier. The algorithm analyses the whole slide image and identifies all glands in the biopsy and classifies them. The identified glands are then presented to the pathologist in a sorted order that is diagnostically relevant. The steps of the workflow are

1. Select the case to be reviewed
2. Select the PIN-4 slide to be reviewed
3. The system does a whole slide analysis of the PIN-4 slide.
4. The system presents all the glands that have been identified and in an order that allows the pathologist to review all glands very efficiently
5. The system presents the gland class during review and also presents additional measurements on the glands and tumor.

# 3     Segmentation, Identification and Classification

The key phases of the analysis in Prostate PIN-4 CAD algorithm are

1. Segment the glands from the other stromal areas
2. Identify glands such that care is taken to make sure glands from two different classes are not merged and identified as a single gland
3. Classify the gland as adenocarcinoma, HGPIN, and Benign

## 3.1     Gland Segmentation

Segmenting glands out of microscopy/biopsy images is a challenging problem for several reasons. Segmentation of the glands when the glands are well formed is relatively easy. However, the regions of interest are cancerous tumor areas. Such areas rarely have well formed and separated glands. Glands come in a wide variety of irregular shapes and sizes. Furthermore, the images are typically full of distracting structures and have varying background that can result in poor segmentation. Sometimes the manual identification of individual glands is also challenging. We explored two different segmentation approaches:

1. Unsupervised Color Segmentation
2. Learning based Classifier

Traditional segmentation algorithms are fully unsupervised and are therefore in general unable to classify a segmented region as being a gland or other tissue. It has been observed that segmentation performance is very poor if higher level information is not taken into account. On the other hand, statistical learning methods from the object detection literature, such as the Viola-Jones face detector [6], cannot be readily applied to this problem because the object of interest are deformable and come in a wide variety of shapes and sizes. Nevertheless, we would like to take advantage of the vast advances made in this field in recent years (e.g. pedestrian detection accuracy has improved dramatically over the last decade [7]).

**Unsupervised Color Segmentation.** Our approach to segmentation and identification follows an iterative multiphase process. In the first phase, we segment and extract candidate gland regions using just the color staining. The brown regions are typically the basal layer cells. However, regions with non-specific brown staining can also occur. The deep blue regions are the epithelial cells within the glands but also the stromal cells nuclei. The red regions appear within the cytoplasm of the epithelial cells of the glands. Non-specific red staining also appears in some areas of the biopsy. The light regions within the tissue regions are typically are the candidate lumen regions of the gland.

Color segmentation is done in a CIE L*a*b space. A constrained K-means clustering technique in the three dimensional color space is used to segment the image into clusters that broadly correspond to *Brown, Blue, Red,* and *Light* colored regions. Initial three-dimensional color vector seed values for *Brown, Blue, Red* and *Light* are specified. The convergent color thresholds are constrained to be around the specified initial cluster seeds. We determine the seed color vectors through a calibration step during the training phase of the algorithm. Sample images with known ground truth are used to determine the seed color vectors of the *Red, Brown, Blue* and *Light* clusters. This model is fairly robust within a single lab setting because of the operations followed within the lab quality process. Color segmentation is followed with a connected component blob analysis to extract multiple connected regions. One of the weaknesses of pixel-level clustering methods is that the context and any top-level information about the shape priors and size are ignored in the segmentation process.

**Learning based Classifier.** Our learning classifier is motivated by the advances in object detection. We turned to a recently published state-of-the-art pedestrian system [7], and applied a similar method for gland segmentation. At a high level, our learning approach can be summarized as follows. We begin by sliding an image patch classifier densely over the input image. In the first step, the patch classifier outputs the likelihood that the pixel in the center of a given patch belongs to a gland (see figure 2). In the next step, the resulting classifier response map is passed into an efficient segmentation algorithm.

The first component of our system involves an image patch classifier. To train this classifier, we labeled 8 training images by hand. Labeling was done by outlining all glands in these images. From this, we extracted 5,000 positive image patches (i.e. patches extracted from the gland regions), and 15,000 negative image patches (i.e. patches extracted from the non-gland regions). The patch size was fixed to 61x61. The classifier we trained was AdaBoost with decision stumps

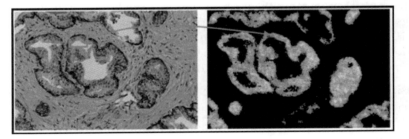

**Fig. 2.** A sliding window classifier is used to predict the likelihood of belonging to a gland for each pixel. Left image is the input image, and the right image is the resulting response map

as the weak classifiers. The features used were Haar-like features computed over the following channels: LUV color channels, gradient magnitude, histogram of gradient orientation channels, and a local standard deviation channel. For more details we refer the reader to [7].

**Graph-Based Segmentation.** The result of applying the trained classifier to a novel input image is a response map where for each pixel we have a likelihood that that pixel belongs to a gland (e.g. the right image figure 2). In the second phase of our system, we pass this response image into an efficient graph based segmentation algorithm described in [8]. Note that segmenting the response image is much easier than segmenting the original input image. Furthermore, the class (i.e. gland or non-gland) of each segment can subsequently be determined using the response image.

Qualitative results on novel test images are shown in figure 3. The trained classifier works well on picking up gland regions even though there is a high variability of appearances (colors and textures). Notice that, unlike pixel color clustering approach, this approach does not rely on a particular stain or color - glands that are not are surrounded by brown staining are picked up just as well as glands that are. One of the challenges we need to address is that the method sometimes merges two glands together incorrectly.

## 3.2   Gland Identification and Classification

In this step, the objective is to either to merge or split the regions output by the segmentation process into gland objects.

**Adjacency analysis:** The non-connected candidate clusters are ranked by its probability to be part of a gland. Candidate regions are analyzed within the context of the adjacent regions. Regions are combined by associating the candidate regions with a gland using the geometric relations between the different parts of the gland. The step results in candidate glands.

**Merging and Splitting:** Candidate glands are split into two or merged into a single gland. The splitting and merging criterion is based on identification of the basal layer and intervening stromal regions. Further, we do a risk based analysis for the sensitivity of splitting or merging. If the class of two candidate regions are the same then merging them carries no risk. Similarly if splitting does not change the class of either one of the candidate regions then there is no risk associated with the split. For merges and splits where the classification changes, additional analysis is done to improve the probability of the gland identification. This is done by the improved detection of stromal and basal regions.

**Classification:** Once the identification is completed the classification of the glands is not too complex. The classification criterion is

1. If gland has only the brown basal staining then the tumor is benign
2. If gland has both the red Racemace and the brown basal staining then it is classified as HGPIN
3. If gland has only the red Racemace then it is classified as adinocarcinoma.

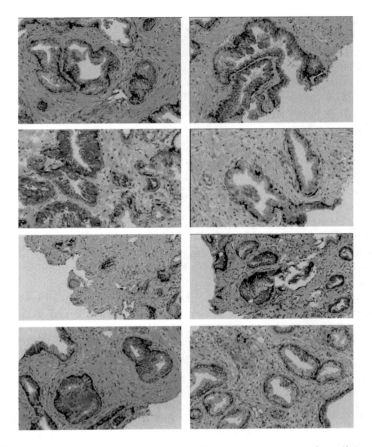

**Fig. 3.** Above Figure shows example results of our system on test (novel) images. See text for details.

## 4   Experiments

We have conducted some experiments with pathologists in the loop to evaluate the effectiveness of our automated CAD algorithm for Prostate PIN4 analysis. Fifty formalin-fixed, paraffin-embedded prostate biopsy cases, each consisting of corresponding H&E and PIN-4 stained slides were selected. These cases were part of a routine workflow in a pathology practice. This ensures that there is no selection bias for the study. DAB chromagen was used to visualize the p63 and HMW cytokeratin antibodies, and AEC chromagen was used to visualize the P504S antibody. Slides were scanned at 20x magnification on the BioImagene iScan Slide Scanner. Manual interpretation (manual digital read) was performed on a computer monitor that allowed the pathologist to view whole slide images at magnifications from 1x to 40x. After a one-week wash-out period, the same cases were reviewed using the PIN-4 image analysis algorithm and BioImagene

Virtuoso software for selected regions of interest. For manual scoring, cases were categorized as benign, HGPIN, atypical/ASAP or adenocarcinoma. For automated analysis, the algorithm categorized cases as benign, HGPIN or adenocarcinoma. Some of the representative samples are presented in figures 4-6 below. We present samples from each one of the classes. Note that the H&E image and the IHC image are not of the same tissue section but are from the same tissue block (serial sections) therefore there is a gross gland level correspondence but no cell level correspondence.

In Figure 4 we present the case of a benign tumor. The pathologist examines the H&E image and suspects a cancer tumor based on the gland morphology and structural arrangements. The PIN-4 test is ordered that is carried out on a serial section from the same block from which the H&E was generated. In 4.b the algorithm has segmented and identified the individual glands. All glands have been classified as benign (therefore outlined with green). Figure 5 presents the case of a high grade prostatic intraepithelial neoplasia (HGPIN) which are suspected to be the precursors to adenocarcinoma. The automated algorithm identifies the glands and correctly classifies them as HGPIN (therefore marking them with a yellow outline). Finally, Figure 6 presents the case of an adenocarcinoma. The CAD algorithm has correctly segmented and identified the individual glands. The classification is that of adenocarcinoma (therefore outlined with red). Note

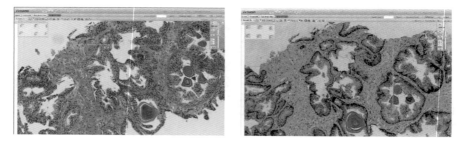

**Fig. 4.** Examples of benign prostate biopsies stained with H&E with corresponding area in PIN-4 IHC. The benign glands are outlined in green in the PIN-4 stained image as a result of the CAD analysis.

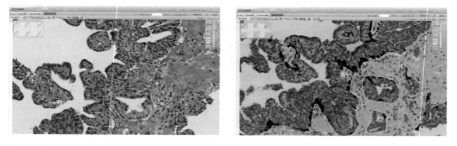

**Fig. 5.** Example of HGPIN stained with H&E and corresponding PIN-4 IHC. The HGPIN glands detected and classified by the CAD algorithm are outlined in yellow.

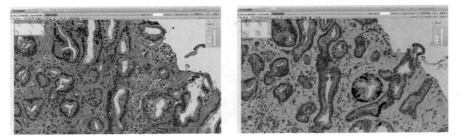

**Fig. 6.** Example of adenocarcinoma stained with H&E and corresponding PIN-4 IHC. The adenocarcinoma glands detected and classified by the CAD algorithm are outlined in red.

that there is one gland in the mix that is actually benign. It is important for the CAD algorithm to not merge this gland with the surrounding glands or the diagnosis will be incorrect.

## 5    Results

We present the results of our experiments that compare the final automated classification of the whole slide v/s the manual classification. The comparative results are based only on gland segmentation produced by the unsupervised color segmentation followed with gland identification and classification. In a future work, we plan to do a similar experiment using the gland segmentation results generated from the image patch classifier approach.

Although comparison of only the final diagnostic results hides a large number of misclassifications, mis-identifications and erroneous segmentation, this is the metric that is of final relevance to the final practice of pathology. We are in the process of developing a large ground truth dataset that includes the manual segmentation and gland identification for the whole slide images. With such datasets we will be able to provide quantitative accuracy results of the gland identification and segmentation procedures.

The first set of tabulated results (Table 1) shows comparison of manual read v/s automated scoring of benign cases and abnormal cases. Benign cases include cases that are classified as Benign and HGPIN. Abnormal cases are adenocarcinoma and atypical/ASAP. Note that the automated algorithm did not classify ASAPs but the manual reads did use the ASAP category. As the table indicates, there was only one case where the manual classification was Abnormal while the CAD analysis algorithm reported Benign. This is the case of ASAP that was not recognized by the CAD algorithm (figure 7). In the future we plan to include another class for ASAP. We have not included ASAP in the current experiment as they are relatively rare and difficult to get sufficient training samples. As seen in the result below we are seeing a concordance of 98% between the manual and the automated classifications.

**Table 1.** Manual digital read vs. CAD analysis for interpretation of benign versus abnormal PIN-4 IHC staining. Benign classification includes benign and HGPIN cases. Abnormal classification includes atypical/ASAP and adenocarcinoma cases. Concordance = 98%.

|  |  | Image Analysis | |
|---|---|---|---|
|  |  | Benign | Abnormal |
| Manual Digital Read | Benign | 29 | 0 |
|  | Abnormal | 1 | 20 |

**Fig. 7.** Example of an atypical focus (ASAP) in a prostate biopsy stained with H&E and the corresponding detection in PIN4. The analysis result was adenocarcinoma.

**Table 2.** Manual digital read vs. CAD for interpretation of benign versus benign/HGPIN PIN-4 IHC staining. Benign classification includes benign cases while benign/HGPIN classification includes benign cases with HGPIN. Concordance = 90%.

|  |  | Image Analysis | |
|---|---|---|---|
|  |  | Benign | Benign+HGPIN |
| Manual Digital Read | Benign | 16 | 1 |
|  | Benign+HGPIN | 2 | 10 |

In table 2 below we present the results of the comparison of manual read v/s automated scoring of Benign cases and HGPIN cases. The concordance between the manual read and the automated CAD is lower in this case. We have a 90% concordance. The reason is that the racemace staining is difficult to use and therefore there is a big variation in the staining intensity. When the glands are small, as in the case of HGPIN, the staining variation causes the recognition of the red staining to be error prone.

In summary:

- There is close agreement between manual digital reading and image analysis for interpretation of PIN-4 IHC staining
- CAD image analysis correctly categorizes glands into benign, HGPIN and malignant categories in most cases

- There is a 98% concordance between manual and automated classification for benign (benign and HGPIN) vs. abnormal diagnoses (adenocarcinoma and atypical) (refer to Table 1)
- There is a 90% concordance between manual and automated classification for benign vs. benign/HGPIN (benign and HGPIN) diagnoses (refer to Table 2)
- The CAD image analysis algorithm does not currently have an atypical category for small numbers of glands lacking basal cell staining. This explains the handful of cases where the manual interpretation was benign or atypical, but the IA interpretation was adenocarcinoma.

## 6  Discussions

Image analysis based CAD is a useful adjunctive tool to aid the pathologist in the interpretation of PIN-4 IHC studies. The PIN-4 algorithm can identify glands in three categories, and there is a high degree of concordance between manual interpretation and automated image analysis. To our knowledge, this is the first example of an algorithm to incorporate three color image analysis of an IHC cocktail.

Planned future versions of the PIN-4 algorithm will include an atypical/ASAP category, perform more accurate analysis based on integrating with H&E and calibration slides.

As digital pathology is increasingly adopted within the pathology practice, CAD algorithms for assisting the pathologist will enable a fundamental change to the practice of pathology. In the early phases of the adoption we observe that only a limited number of CAD algorithms provide the pathologist the additional information that helps them with certainty of diagnosis. An area of increasing utility is the optimization of workflow through the use of CAD algorithms. If the system is able to preprocess the images for the pathologist and presents the information in the order that is diagnostically relevant, the time to derive an accurate and correct diagnosis will be significantly reduced. Further, the directed review of the pathology slides will result in lower fatigue which will improve the quality of the pathology practice.

The PIN-4 algorithm developed by BioImagene is one such algorithm that has been adopted by the practicing pathologist to help in the diagnosis of adenocarcinoma in prostate needle biopsies. The usefulness of PIN-4 is still being studied and a final equivocal decision has not been arrived at in the community. However, we feel that the use of PIN-4 in the preprocessing of the whole slide image has the potential to dramatically alter the protocol of prostate screening process. The discussion of the usefulness of PIN-4 at that time will take a new dimension that will have to take into account the automated screening aspect of the test.

## References

1. Weng Leong Ng, V., et al.: Is Triple Immunostaining With 34E12, p63, and Racemase in Prostate Cancer Advantageous? Am. J. Clin. Pathol. 127, 248–253 (2007)
2. Ayala, A.G., et al.: Prostatic Intraepithelial Neoplasia: Recent Advances. Arch. Pathol. Lab. Med. 131(8), 1257–1266

3. Molinie, V., et al.: Diagnostic utility of a p63/alpha-methyl-CoA-racemase (p504s) cocktail in atypical foci in the prostate. Mod. Pathol. 17(10), 1180–1190 (2004)
4. Freeimage Open Source Project: http://freeimage.sourceforge.net/
5. OpenCV Library Open Source Project: http://sourceforge.net/projects/opencvlibrary/
6. Viola, P., Jones, M.: Robust Realtime Face Recognition. International Journal of Computer Vision 57(2), 137–154 (2004)
7. P. Dollar, Z. Tu, P. Perona and S. Belongie: Integral Channel Features. In: BMVC 2009 (2009)
8. Felzenszwalb, P.F., Huttenlocher, D.P.: Efficient Graph-Based Image Segmentation. International Journal on Computer Vision 59(2), 167–181 (2004)

# Augmented Reality Image Guidance in Minimally Invasive Prostatectomy

Daniel Cohen[1,4], Erik Mayer[1,4], Dongbin Chen[1], Ann Anstee[3], Justin Vale[4], Guang-Zhong Yang[2], Ara Darzi[1], and Philip 'Eddie' Edwards[1,2]

[1] Department of Surgery and Cancer
Imperial College, London, UK
[2] Department of Computing,
Imperial College, London, UK
[3] Radiology Department and [4] Urology Department, St Mary's Hospital,
Imperial College NHS Trust, London, UK
daniel.cohen@imperial.ac.uk, eddie.edwards@imperial.ac.uk

**Abstract.** This paper presents our work aimed at providing augmented reality (AR) guidance of robot-assisted laparoscopic surgery (RALP) using the da Vinci system. There is a good clinical case for guidance due to the significant rate of complications and steep learning curve for this procedure. Patients who were due to undergo robotic prostatectomy for organ-confined prostate cancer underwent preoperative 3T MRI scans of the pelvis. These were segmented and reconstructed to form 3D images of pelvic anatomy. The reconstructed image was successfully overlaid onto screenshots of the recorded surgery post-procedure. Surgeons who perform minimally-invasive prostatectomy took part in a user-needs analysis to determine the potential benefits of an image guidance system after viewing the overlaid images. All surgeons stated that the development would be useful at key stages of the surgery and could help to improve the learning curve of the procedure and improve functional and oncological outcomes. Establishing the clinical need in this way is a vital early step in development of an AR guidance system. We have also identified relevant anatomy from preoperative MRI. Further work will be aimed at automated registration to account for tissue deformation during the procedure, using a combination of transrectal ultrasound and stereoendoscopic video.

**Keywords:** MRI scan prostate, image guidance, augmented reality, robot-assisted laparoscopic prostatectomy (RALP).

## 1 Introduction

### 1.1 Clinical Background

Prostate cancer, the most common cancer in men in the UK, accounted for 9157 deaths in 2008 [1]. 30201 new diagnoses of the disease were made in 2007, and the

A. Madabhushi et al. (Eds.): Prostate Cancer Imaging 2010, LNCS 6367, pp. 101–110, 2010.

incidence of prostate cancer is likely to increase due to an aging population [2]. The 5 year survival rate is 71% which is aided by accurate surgical intervention and early detection using prostate-specific antigen. Radical prostatectomy is a well established treatment for organ confined prostate cancer and confers survival benefit [3].

There are three common methods for performing a radical prostatectomy. The longest-established method is open surgery, either by retropubic or perineal approach, which was first described in 1905 by H Young [4]. The description and uptake of anatomic prostatectomy in the late 1970s refined the technique of the surgery. Open surgery is still the gold standard procedure for radical prostatectomy, although it is complicated by higher rates of blood loss and a longer hospital stay than for minimally-invasive procedures [5].

Minimally invasive radical prostatectomy can be performed by laparoscopic or robot-assisted laparoscopic methods. Laparoscopic surgery increased in popularity in the late 1990s and in the hands of an experienced surgeon, can deliver good patient outcomes. However, the procedure remains technically complex and has a long and difficult learning curve due to the constraints of operating with a laparoscopic system, such as the absence of haptic feedback, a reduced range of instrument motion, and 2-dimensional visualisation during the procedure [5].

Robot-assisted laparoscopic surgery is a further advance and has been increasing in popularity in the last ten years, with estimates that over 70% of prostatectomies in the United States are now performed this way. Systems such as the da Vinci Robot have added benefits to conventional laparoscopic surgery, including 3-dimensional vision, improved ergonomics, motion-scaling and tremor loss, and an increased range of motion for surgical instruments. Despite the rapid and costly uptake of RALP, there is debate as to which modality of prostatectomy confers the most benefit to patients, as the negative outcomes of positive surgical margins, functional impairment (erectile dysfunction, urinary incontinence) due to nerve damage and iatrogenic injury to surrounding structures are equally prevalent across the surgical modalities. Proponents of robot-assisted surgery claim it is superior to open or laparoscopic techniques. However, these claims are controversial and based on low quality evidence [5,6]. It is hoped that the forthcoming LopERA trial in the United Kingdom will add high quality evidence to this debate [6].

However, of all the techniques described above, RALP has been purported to have the greatest potential for improving outcomes in the future, due to ongoing research and developments of this relatively new technology [7].

The addition of augmented reality (AR) to robotic prostatectomy will enhance and potentially standardise the accuracy of surgery. Having the cancerous growth 'visible' by means of AR may aid in complete macroscopic excision, particularly in the difficult region of the prostatic apex where positive cancerous margins are most common, resulting in improved oncological cure. Display of surrounding anatomy could result in improved neurovascular bundle and sphincter preservation and guide bladder neck dissection, improving the potency and urinary continence rates achievable after RALP. The real time display of adjacent organs will reduce the potential for intraoperative morbidity such as rectal injury [8].

The learning curve for robotic techniques has also been identified as a factor in surgical outcome [9]. Initial reports suggest a shorter learning curve for robot-assisted radical prostatectomy over conventional laparoscopic radical prostatectomy, with the advantage that prior laparoscopic experience may not be required [10]. However there is still a significant learning curve for robot-assisted radical prostatectomy which can be further shortened by improving the anatomical orientation within the male pelvis using AR.

We describe our research to develop image guidance technology for RALP in order to improve surgical outcomes.

## 1.2 Background to Augmented Reality

Image guidance is becoming an accepted tool for applications in neurosurgery, ENT, maxillofacial surgery and orthopaedics [11], where the operations are close to bone. Here there can be rigid alignment of the image to the physical space of the patient. Within the abdomen, image guidance has been proposed to aid gastrointestinal, biliary and pancreatic surgery [12].

The use of image guidance in urological surgery is as yet uncommon. There has been one report of an AR guided adrenalectomy and one of image guided partial nephrectomy [13,14]. Both these studies used preoperative CT scans to define anatomy intraoperatively.

Transrectal ultrasound real-time guidance has been utilised in both open and laparoscopic radical prostatectomy. The authors suggested that this modality was helpful in identification of prostate margins and neurovascular bundles during surgery [15]. However, this technology has not become widely used, which may be due to the technical challenges of intraoperative ultrasonography, the need to have a ultrasonographer present throughout the procedure and the lack of high quality evidence showing improvements in patient outcome.

As yet, no studies have utilised preoperative MRI scans in this anatomical region for image-guided surgery. MRI is the imaging modality of choice in prostate cancer, as it enables clear identification of intraprostatic anatomy and margins. These are both poorly defined on CT [16]. The use of MRI may also enable clear delineation of the neurovascular bundles running adjacent to the prostate. Damage to these structures during a prostatectomy is thought to be responsible for the functional problems that are reported after surgery.

Combining intraoperative transrectal ultrasound scans with preoperative MRI may enable real-time image overlay during prostatectomy. However, transrectal probes may alter the shape of the prostate, which could have implications during both image reconstruction and overlay.

This project aims to bring AR image guidance to radical prostatectomy by utilising preoperative MRI imaging. AR surgical guidance has the potential to reduce morbidity and improve outcome for prostate cancer patients. This project will build such a system and begin to evaluate its clinical efficacy for prostatectomy.

## 2  Methods

### 2.1  MRI Scanning, Segmentation and Image Overlay

Ten patients with histologically proven early stage prostate cancer were listed for robotic prostatectomy at St Mary's Hospital, Imperial College Healthcare NHS Trust, London. This cohort all underwent conventional 3T CUBE MRI scans of the pelvis preoperatively. Three patients also underwent pre-biopsy endoanal 3T CUBE MRI scans to determine the effects on prostate deformation and enable comparison with conventional scans. None of these patients has proceeded to prostatectomy as yet, therefore these scans have not undergone segmentation and overlay.

An anatomical protocol was established to guide the segmentation. The following structures were deemed important to identify as a minimum requirement: prostate, bladder, urethra, vas deferens, seminal vesicles, rectum, neurovascular bundles and ureters. Other structures were identified as deemed necessary at the time of segmentation. The scans underwent manual segmentation and reconstruction by a specialist MRI consultant radiologist to form a 3 dimensional reconstruction.

Intraoperative recording of the robotic prostatectomies took place via a stereo-recording system connected to the standard equipment stack in theatre. All patients were consented pre-MRI and pre-surgery for their images to be used for the purposes of this study.

Post-operatively, the 3-dimensional reconstructed view was aligned to the console view for the purpose of retrospective evaluation by the surgeon.

### 2.2  Establishing the Need for an Image Guidance System

The theoretical benefits of image guidance have been discussed above. However, there is no qualitative data in the literature to support its development or to gain further insight into the uses, benefits and applicability of a system. A user-needs analysis was therefore performed. This was undertaken by means of semi-structured interviews on surgeons who perform minimally-invasive prostatectomy (figure 1). The stages of minimally invasive prostatectomy have been described elsewhere [17]; this structure was used to make the interview systematic. The interviews were transcribed in real-time and then underwent qualitative analysis to determine the perceived technical difficulties of the current procedure and the future benefits of an image guidance system.

### 2.2.1  MRI Scanning Modality

Fig. 2(a) shows a conventional 3T scan, clearly showing the anatomical boundaries of the prostate and surrounding anatomy. By contrast, Fig. 2(b) shows an MRI scan taken using an endoanal coil. Comparison of these images reveals subtle differences. The endoanal MRI image shows deformation of the prostate due to the ano-rectal probe, and more defined intraprostatic anatomy. As well as providing better contrast in this region the use of the endoanal coil may closer mimic the tissue deformation due to intraoperative transrectal ultrasound should this become our method of soft tissue tracking.

**Augmented Reality Guidance for Robotic Prostatectomy**
**What do Surgeons want from a system?**

1.  What type of minimally-invasive prostatectomy do you perform?
2.  How many have you performed?
3.  Do you follow the 9 stage system previously described?
4.  Do you think an image guidance system would be helpful, and if so, how?
5.  What complications could an image guidance system help to avoid?
6.  Are there any other steps in the procedure where use of image guidance might be helpful?
7.  What are the requirements for successful implementation from a surgical point of view?

|  | What are the technical challenges at each stage? | What structures/anatomy would be useful to identify at each stage? How might an image guidance system help? |
|---|---|---|
| 1. Incision of peritoneum | | |
| 2. Incision of endopelvic fascia | | |
| 3. Ligation of dorsal vein complex | | |
| 4. Dissection of the bladder neck | | |
| 5. Seminal vesicle dissection | | |
| 6. Denonvilliers posterior dissection | | |
| 7. Nerve-sparing right and left | | |
| 8. Mobilising apex | | |
| 9. Anastamosis | | |

**Fig. 1.** Semi-structured interviews for urological surgeons

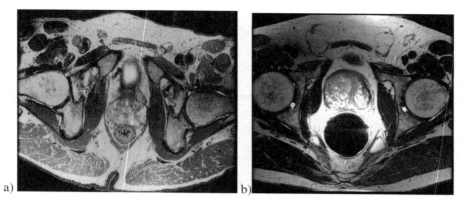

**Fig. 2.** Example MRI scans - conventional (a) and with an endoanal coil (b)

### 2.2.2 MRI Segmentation and Image Overlay

MRI scans were successfully segmented and reconstructed in 3D. Relevant anatomy was identified and coloured. The images were then calibrated and overlaid onto still images of a recorded robotic prostatectomy.

The combined images show the anatomy of the pelvis from the viewpoint of the operating surgeon. The images are scaled to reflect the magnification seen intraoperatively.

Fig. 3 shows the appearance of the pelvic cavity at the beginning of the procedure. There is a significant pneumoperitoneum moving the abdominal wall anteriorly and therefore increasing the space for the robotic instruments to work. In Fig. 3(b) the overlay demonstrates segmented and reconstructed pelvic organs from the preoperative MRI scan that have been overlaid onto the operative image. The prostate (green), seminal vesicles (pink) and left sided neurovascular bundle (yellow) can be seen along with the pelvic bony structure (white/grey). The bladder has been removed

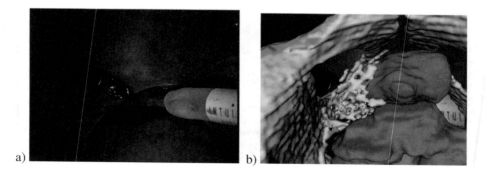

**Fig. 3.** The pelvic cavity at the beginning of the procedure – the operative view (a) and the same view with overlay (b)

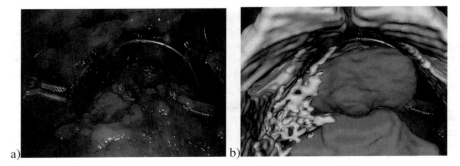

**Fig. 4.** Dorsal vein complex without (a) and with (b) overlay

from the image as it was full during the preoperative MRI and occludes the other structures when overlaid. Furthermore, during the procedure the patient has a urinary catheter and therefore the bladder is decompressed. Note that these images do not reflect the pneumoperitoneum and therefore the structures are not completely aligned.

Fig. 4 shows the dorsal vein complex about to be ligated by the surgeon. The needle is clearly visible in the screenshot. Again, the pneumoperitoneum makes accurate overlay difficult other than for the bony pelvis. Interestingly, the neurovascular bundle is not clearly visible on the screenshot, but is obvious on the augmented reality overlay.

### 2.3 Establishing the Requirements and Use of an Image-Guided System

Initial results of the questionnaire were encouraging. All surgeons believed that the system would be useful, although none believed that the system was of any benefit for stages 1, 2 and 9. All surgeons felt that the system would be of particular benefit to novice robotic surgeons and could help to accelerate the learning curve.

In stage 3, visualisation of the depth of the dorsal venous complex and position of the urethra was felt to be a potentially useful addition to aid needle placement and avoid urethral injury. Most surgeons felt that image guidance in stage 4 could help to preserve the bladder neck if required, and also prevent inadvertent entry into a large middle prostatic lobe. Seminal vesicle dissection was felt to be a technically challenging procedure (stage 5), although image guidance was not universally felt to be of help, other than initial location of the vesicles. One surgeon noted that neurovascular bundles did run close to seminal vesicles, and visualisation of these prior to dissection could help avoid iatrogenic injury. All surgeons agreed that stage 6, which commences with a dissection of Denonvillers fascia, could be made safer by visualising the rectum posterior to the fascia and guiding the depth of dissection. Rectal injury is a concern during this part of the procedure.

The development of an image guidance system was felt to be of greatest benefit in stages 7 and 8. High precision surgery in these areas can result in improved functional and oncological outcomes, by preservation of the neurovascular bundles and complete excision of a cancer. Stage 7 begins with the division of the lateral pedicles. Surgeons felt that identification of the neurovascular bundle in relation to the lateral pedicle would be a very useful development, and would aid nerve-sparing. One surgeon commented that anatomical differences between patients at this stage of the surgery made nerve-sparing a potentially difficult procedure, and one that image guidance could make much safer. Stage 8 involves complete dissection of the prostate down to the apex. Image guidance was felt to be useful here on two grounds. Firstly, the image guidance could show the cancerous tumour within the prostate and therefore guide complete excision during surgery, making a positive cancer margin less likely. Secondly, there was concern that surgeons at present may injure the external sphincter during the apical dissection, which image guidance could help to avoid.

More generally, surgeons stated that operative complications that could be avoided were any iatrogenic injury and inadvertent incision of the prostate. One surgeon commented that the system must work in real time when developed, in order to avoid lengthening the surgery.

## 3  Discussion and Future Work

We have demonstrated the capability of using preoperative MRI images to form a 3 dimensional anatomical model. Furthermore, we have enabled successful overlay and alignment of the reconstructed MRI image onto the stereo view that the surgeon would see during a robotic prostatectomy, thus giving graphical representation of intraoperative anatomy. We have identified which anatomical structures are useful to identify at certain key stages of the surgery. This is a vital stage in establishing the clinical need for image guidance in RALP.

There are a number of technical developments in progress. We are researching methods to provide a smooth and automated segmentation of the 3D MRI scan. Clearly the soft tissue deformation due to pneumoperitoneum and surgical mobilisation currently results in suboptimal registration. This challenge needs to be overcome to enable accurate image guidance intraoperatively. A registration technique that does not take account of the surgery-induced anatomical deformities will be of little use in improving surgical accuracy. In particular, preservation of the neurovascular bundles (aiding urinary continence and erectile function) and accurate mobilisation of the prostatic apex (aiding complete oncological resection) require high surgical precision, which can only be promoted by an accurate, deformable, image guidance system.

We are researching possible methods of maintaining alignment in the presence of soft tissue deformation using transrectal ultrasound to follow the motion of the prostate and nearby structures. We have anticipated that transrectal intraoperative ultrasound would significantly alter the shape of the prostate due to direct pressure. For this reason we are investigating whether the MRI should be performed with an endo-anal coil (rather than a pelvic coil) in order that the soft tissue deformation is similar to that when the transrectal ultrasound probe is inserted. We are performing further research into the use of the steroendocsopic video to reconstruct the viewed surface for intraoperative registration. For accurate live-overlay to take place the problem of soft tissue motion needs to be addressed.

It is expected that the overall system will lead to two major improvements in practice. Firstly, we expect both oncological and functional outcome improvements in patients who undergo robotic prostatectomy for early-stage prostate cancer as a result of image guidance. Secondly, we anticipate that the learning curve of the procedure will be improved for novice surgeons. Both of these developments would be of significant benefit to prostate cancer patients.

# Acknowledgements

We are grateful to the radiology, radiography and theatre staff at St Mary's, Imperial Colleg Healthcare NHS Trust as well as the other members of the Department of Surgery and Cancer at Imperial for their advice and cooperation throughout the project. Particular thanks go to Cancer Research UK for funding this work under project number C24520/A8087.

# References

1. Office of national statistics. Mortality statistics. Series DR08 (2008)
2. Office of national statistics, Cancer Statistsics registrations. Series MB1, no. 38 (2007)
3. Holmberg, L., Bill-Axelson, A., Helgesen, F., Salo, J.O., Folmerz, P., Haggman, M., Andersson, S., Spangberg, A., Busch, C., Nordling, S., Palmgren, J., Adami, H., Johansson, J., Norlen, B.J.: A randomized trial comparing radical prostatectomy with watchful waiting in early prostate cancer. N. Engl. J. Med. 347, 781–789 (2002)
4. Young, H.: The early diagnosis and radical cure of carcinoma of the prostate. Being a study of 40 cases and presentation of a radical operation which was carried out in four cases (1905); J. Urol. 167, 939–946 (2002)
5. Ficarra, V., Novara, G., Artbani, W., et al.: Retropubic, Laparoscopic, and Robot-Assisted Radical Prostatectomy: A Systematic Review and Cumulative Analysis of Comparative Studies. Eur. Urol. 55, 1037–1063 (2009)
6. Kang, D., Hardee, M., Fesperman, S., Stoffs, T., Dahm, P.: Low Quality of Evidence for Robot-Assisted Laparoscopic Prostatectomy: Results of a Systematic Review of the Published Literature. Eur. Urol. 57, 930–937 (2010)
7. Graefen, M.: Low Quality of Evidence for Robot-Assisted Laparoscopic Prostatectomy: A problem not only in the robotic literature. Eur. Urol. 57, 938–940 (2010)
8. Ukimura, O.: Image-guided surgery in minimally invasive urology. Current Opinion in Urology 20, 136–140 (2010)
9. Van Appledorn, S., Bouchier-Hayes, D., Agarwal, D., Costello, A.J.: Robotic laparoscopic radical prostatectomy: Setup and procedural techniques after 150 cases. Urology 67, 364–367 (2006)
10. Peter, E., Lee, D.I., Ahlering, T., Clayman, R.V.: Robotic revelation: Laparoscopic radical prostatectomy by a nonlaparoscopic surgeon. J. Am. Coll. Surg. 197, 693–696 (2003)
11. Aquilina, K., Edwards, P.J., Strong, A.J.: Principles and practice of image-guided neurosurgery. In: Moore, M.A. (ed.) Springer Specialist Surgical Series: Neurosurger. Springer, Heidelberg (2003)
12. Sugimoto, M., Yasuda, H., Koda, K., Suzuki, M., et al.: Image overlay navigation by markerless surface registration in gastrointestinal, hepatobiliary and pancreatic surgery. J. Hepatobiliary Pancreat. Surg. (2009), doi:10.1007/s00534-009-0199-y
13. Marescaux, J., Rubino, F., Arenas, M., Mutter, D., Soler, L.: Augmented-reality assisted laparoscopic adrenalectomy. J. Am. Med. Assoc. 292(18), 2214–2215 (2004)
14. Teber, D., Guven, S., Simpfendorfer, T., Baumhauer, M., Guven, E., Yencilek, F., Gozen, A., Rassweiler, J.: Augmented Reality: A new tool to improve surgical accuracy during laparoscopic partial nephrectomy? Preliminary In Vitro and In Vivo results. Eur. Urol. 56, 332–338 (2009)

15. Ukimura, O., Magi-Galluzzi, C., Gill, I.: Real-time transrectal ultrasound guidance during laparoscopic radical prostatectomy: impact on surgical margins. J. Urol. 175, 1304–1310 (2006)
16. Fuchsjager, M., Shukla-Dave, A., Akin, O., Barentsz, J., Hricak, H.: Prostate cancer imaging. Acta Radiol. 49, 107–120 (2008)
17. Tewari, A., Peabody, J., Sarle, R., et al.: Technique of da Vinci robot assisted anatomic radical prostatectomy. Urology 60(4), 569–572 (2002)

# Texture Guided Active Appearance Model Propagation for Prostate Segmentation

Soumya Ghose[1,2], Arnau Oliver[1], Robert Martí[1], Xavier Lladó[1],
Jordi Freixenet[1], Joan C. Vilanova[3], and Fabrice Meriaudeau[2]

[1] Computer Vision and Robotics Group, University of Girona, Campus Montilivi,
Edifici P-IV, Av. Lluís Santaló , s/n, 17071 Girona, Spain
[2] Laboratoire Le2I - UMR CNRS 5158, Université de Bourgogne,
12 Rue de la Fonderie, 71200 Le Creusot, France
[3] Girona Magnetic Resonance Imaging Center, Girona, Spain

**Abstract.** Fusion of Magnetic Resonance Imaging (MRI) and Trans
Rectal Ultra Sound (TRUS) images during TRUS guided prostate biopsy
improves localization of the malignant tissues. Segmented prostate in
TRUS and MRI improve registration accuracy and reduce computational
cost of the procedure. However, accurate segmentation of the prostate
in TRUS images can be a challenging task due to low signal to noise
ratio, heterogeneous intensity distribution inside the prostate, and imaging artifacts like speckle noise and shadow. We propose to use texture
features from approximation coefficients of Haar wavelet transform for
propagation of a shape and appearance based statistical model to segment the prostate in a multi-resolution framework. A parametric model
of the propagating contour is derived from Principal Component Analysis of prior shape and texture informations of the prostate from the
training data. The parameters are then modified with prior knowledge
of the optimization space to achieve optimal prostate segmentation. The
proposed method achieves a mean Dice Similarity Coefficient value of
$0.95 \pm 0.01$, and mean segmentation time of $0.72 \pm 0.05$ seconds when
validated on 25 TRUS images, grabbed from video sequences, in a leave-
one-out validation framework. Our proposed model performs computationally efficient accurate prostate segmentation in presence of intensity
heterogeneity and imaging artifacts.

## 1 Introduction

Prostate cancer is a major health problem with more than 670,000 people being
diagnosed every year worldwide [1]. In clinical practice TRUS guided needle
biopsy is performed to diagnose prostate cancer, due to the real time nature of
the imaging system, ease of use, and portability. However, TRUS images have low
signal to noise ratio (SNR) and detection of malignant tissues in TRUS images
is difficult. MR images provide higher contrast for soft tissues of the prostate
that allows a better detection of cancerous tissues. However, interventional MRI

A. Madabhushi et al. (Eds.): Prostate Cancer Imaging 2010, LNCS 6367, pp. 111–120, 2010.
© Springer-Verlag Berlin Heidelberg 2010

guided biopsy is expensive and complicated. Therefore, one solution lies in the fusion of the two imaging modalities to exploit the high quality of MR images in TRUS interventional biopsies. Real-time registration between two dimensional (2D) TRUS video sequence and three dimensional (3D) MR images is necessary for such a process. Registration performed on accurately segmented contour of TRUS and MR images will aid in designing computationally efficient and accurate registration procedures [20]. Thus, real-time accurate 2D segmentation of TRUS images from TRUS video sequence is necessary for the process.

Prostate segmentation in TRUS images is particularly challenging. Low SNR in a TRUS image of prostate reduces the accuracy of intensity based segmentation algorithms. Approaches working on traditional edge detection filters like Sobel, Prewitt are adversely affected with the issues of high noise and low SNR producing discontinuous prostate edges. Heterogeneous intensity distribution inside the prostate is a hindrance in designing a global descriptor. Added to these, shadow artifacts, speckle noise and micro calcification significantly challenges the segmentation of the prostate.

Incorporating prior shape and intensity informations in the segmentation methods improve the prostate segmentation accuracy. In 1998 Cootes et al. [6] provided an efficient framework for combining shape and intensity prior in their Active Appearance Model (AAM). Medina et al. [16] used AAM to segment prostate in Two Dimensional (2D) TRUS images with an overlap ratio of 96%. However, it is argued by Wolstenholme and Taylor [19] that the time complexity involved with AAM is high and is unsuitable for real time procedures. Instead they proposed to use wavelet coefficients of training images for building the AAM. Larsen et al. [14] showed that frequency separation in wavelet transform allowed an edge enhancement that provided better result in terms of segmentation accuracy compared to traditional AAMs. They proposed to use a texture vector comprising the truncated detail and approximation coefficients in multi-resolution framework.

To address the challenges involved with prostate segmentation in 2D TRUS images, we propose a novel AAM that is propagated by the approximation coefficients of Haar wavelet transform in a multi-resolution framework . Compared to the use of intensity as in traditional AAM [6], the use of approximation coefficients of the wavelet transformed image improves the computational time and accuracy of prostate segmentation. The approach is similar to Larsen et al. [14], while deviating from their model of using both detail and approximation coefficients to construct a texture vector for AAM propagation we propose to use the approximation coefficients of the Haar wavelet transformed image. The performance of our method is validated using 25 images captured from TRUS video sequence. Experimental results show that our method is unaffected by low SNR, intensity heterogeneities and micro calcifications inside prostate region and imaging artifacts like shadow and speckle noise.

The rest of the paper is organized as follows. The texture driven AAM is formulated in Section 2 followed by quantitative and qualitative evaluation of our method in Section 3. We finally draw conclusion in Section 4.

## 2 Methods

The proposed method is developed on two major components: the adaptation of AAM and incorporation of texture information. Traditional AAM is presented first followed by a comprehensive discussion of using Haar wavelet in extraction of texture feature to build the model. Finally, the model building and propagation procedure are presented.

### 2.1 Active Appearance Model

AAM provides a compact parametric framework utilizing prior shape and intensity variabilities learned from a training model to segment an unseen test image exploiting the prior knowledge of the nature of the optimization space [14]. The process of building AAM may be partitioned into two separate tasks; building the shape model from the contours and building the appearance model from the intensity distribution inside the manually segmented region. Finally, the two models are combined to produce AAM that incorporates prior knowledge of shape and intensity variabilities.

Generalized Procrustes Analysis (GPA) of the Point Distribution Model (PDM) [5] built from manually segmented contours is used to align the PDM. Principal Component Analysis (PCA) of the aligned PDMs are used to identify the principal components of the variations in shape and suppress redundancy. Intensity distribution are warped into correspondence using a piece wise affine warp and sampled from shape free reference. PCA of the intensity distribution is used to identify the principal components of intensity variations.

The model may be formalized in the following manner. In eq. 2 let $E\{s\}$ and $E\{t\}$ represent the shape and intensity models where $s$ and $t$ are the shape and the intensities of the corresponding training images, $\bar{s}$ and $\bar{t}$ denote the mean shape and intensity respectively, then $\Phi_s$ and $\Phi_t$ contain the first $p$ eigenvectors of the estimated joint dispersion matrix of shape and intensity and $\theta$ represents the corresponding eigenvalues.

$$E\{s\} = \bar{s} + \Phi_s\theta \tag{1}$$
$$E\{t\} = \bar{t} + \Phi_t\theta$$

In addition to the parameters $\theta$, four parameters, two translations, rotation and scale are represented by $\psi$. In order to infer the parameters of $\theta$ and $\psi$ of a previously unseen image, a Gaussian error model between model and pixel intensities is assumed [14]. Furthermore, a linear relationship between changes in parameters and difference between model and image pixel intensities $\Delta t$ is assumed as shown in eq.2

$$\Delta t = X \begin{bmatrix} \Delta\psi \\ \Delta\theta \end{bmatrix} \tag{2}$$

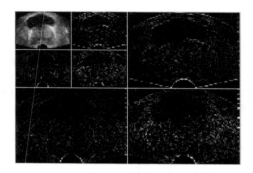

**Fig. 1.** Second level Haar wavelet decomposition of the prostate

$X$ is estimated from weighted averaging over perturbation of model parameters and training examples. Eq.2 is solved in least square manner fitting error as shown in eq.3

$$\begin{bmatrix} \widehat{\psi} \\ \widehat{\theta} \end{bmatrix} = (X^T X)^{-1} X^T \delta t \tag{3}$$

The problem is computationally expensive. To reduce the computational time we propose to use approximation coefficients of Haar wavelet transform. However, this will introduce the additional time requirement of transformation of the image into a new representation. Since the transformation is based on sparse matrix, the computational burden can be considerably reduced as stated in [14].

## 2.2 Texture Analysis Using Haar Wavelets

Wavelets are a family of basis functions that decomposes signal into frequency and time domains. In practice, a set of linear, rank preserving matrix operations are carried out in a convolution scheme to decompose an image by a high pass filter and by a low pass filter into different sub-bands. For a 2D image the high pass filter generates three detail coefficient sub-bands corresponding to horizontal, vertical and the diagonal edges. The approximation sub band obtained from low pass filter, is down-sampled and is further decomposed to analyze the detail and the approximation coefficients at a coarser resolution. The Haar wavelet decomposition of a 2D TRUS image of the prostate is shown in fig.1.

The property of the wavelets that allows to analyze the detail and the approximation coefficients in a multi-resolution framework proves to be a powerful tool for edge and texture analysis [17]. To introduce wavelet coefficients in AAM, we formalize the framework with the used notation. First, let a n-level wavelet transform be denoted by

$$\widehat{w} = \begin{bmatrix} \widehat{a}^T \widehat{u}_1^T \dots \widehat{u}_n^T \end{bmatrix}^T \tag{4}$$

where, $\widehat{a}$ and $\widehat{u}$ represent the approximation and the detail coefficients respectively, and $\widehat{w}$ is the wavelet transformed image [14]. The detail coefficients are suppressed to produce a truncated wavelet basis as

$$b\left(\widehat{w}\right) = C\widehat{w} = \left[\widehat{a}^T 0 \dots 0\right]^T \tag{5}$$

where, $C$ corresponds to a modified identity matrix with the rows corresponding to the detail coefficients removed. The AAM is built on the truncated wavelet basis constituting the texture. The PCA of the texture is given by 6

$$a = \overline{a} + \Phi_a B_w \tag{6}$$

where $\overline{a}$ is the mean of the approximation coefficients, $\Phi_a$ and $B_w$ are the matrices constituting the eigenvectors and their corresponding eigenvalue respectively, that represent the principal components of the approximation coefficients.

Suppressing the high frequency components certainly reduces texture information. However, the texture information that are to be preserved is context dependent. To ensure the uniformity of texture inside the prostate, suppression of the detail coefficients is desirable since, the high gradient energies are minimized. Moreover, speckle noise and micro calcifications, the high frequency components, inside the prostate tissues are considerably reduced by the suppression of the detail coefficients, producing appropriate texture map. Finally, such suppression reduces the computational complexities involved with the fitting of a new image to the model. It is to be noted that, significant texture informations are preserved in the high energy components that are the approximation coefficients [17]. PCA of the approximation coefficients helps us to suppress noise in the underlying texture by preserving the important components only.

### 2.3   Model Building

The model building procedure could be summarized in the following steps,

1. Automatic creation of PDM from the segmented contour using a radial search method.
2. All the PDMs are aligned using GPA.
3. PCA of the aligned contours is done to identify the principal components of the shape variation.
4. Intensities are sampled from each of the aligned PDM.
5. Wavelet transform of the intensities produce the approximation and the detail coefficients.
6. The detail coefficients are suppressed and the approximation coefficients are then used to identify the principle variations of the texture which is used to build the AAM.

Larsen et al. [14] claimed that wavelet decomposition of an image in multiresolution propagates fitting error due to loss of texture information. Therefore, we have adopted wavelet decomposition of the first level and subsequently fitted

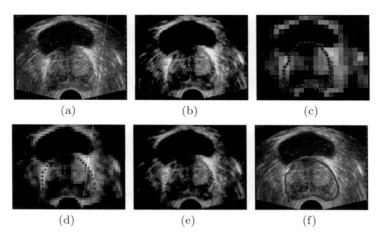

**Fig. 2.** Multi-resolution functioning of the model (a) 2D TRUS image of the prostate, (b) Manual initialization of the mean model (blue contour) by clicking on the center of the prostate, (c) Level 4 segmentation result, (d) Level 3 segmentation result, (e) Level 2 segmentation result, (f) Final segmentation result. Manual segmentation shown with green contour and the red contour show the segmentation achieved.

our model to the approximation coefficients in coarser to finer spatial resolutions to reduce texture dependent fitting error. Multi-resolution fitting of an image improves segmentation accuracy. The multi-resolution functioning of the model is illustrated in fig.2.

It is to be noted that the mean model is initialized by clicking in any position close to the center of the prostate decided on visual inspection. The mean model initialization and subsequent multi-resolution segmentations are produced based on the approximation coefficients of the Haar wavelet.

## 3   Experimental Results

We have validated the accuracy and robustness of our approach on a series of 25 prostate ultrasound images using leave-one-out evaluation strategy. The images of resolution $538 \times 418$ are grabbed from TRUS video sequences (acquired with a Siemens Aquson). Our method was implemented in Matlab 7 on a Intel Core 2 Duo T5250 processor of 1.5 Ghz processor speed and 2 GB RAM. We have used most of the popular prostate segmentation evaluation metrics in order to evaluate our approach. The average values for all the 25 images show, Dice similarity coefficient DSC value of $0.95 \pm 0.01$, 95% Hausdorff Distance (HD) of $5.08 \pm 1.18$ mm, Mean Absolute Distance (MAD) of $1.48 \pm 0.36$ mm, Maximum distance (MaxD) of $5.01 \pm 1.13$ mm, specificity of $0.92 \pm 0.02$ and sensitivity value of $0.998 \pm 0.001$ with a mean segmentation time of $0.72 \pm 0.05$ seconds.

For a qualitative analysis of our method we have presented the 25 figures used for validation with green contours depicting the ground truth and the red contours indicating the segmented prostates as shown in fig.3.

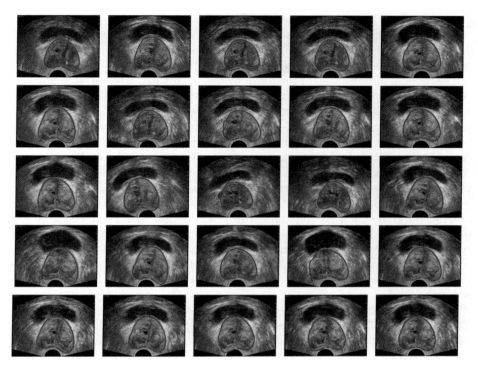

**Fig. 3.** Qualitative segmentation results. The green contour gives the manual segmentation and the red contour gives the obtained result.

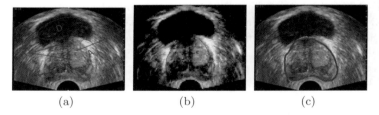

(a)                          (b)                          (c)

**Fig. 4.** (a)Prostate artifacts in TRUS image of the prostate, A=Low SNR, B=Micro-Calcification, C=Intensity difference inside prostate region, D=Shadow Artifacts, E=Speckle Noise. (b) Manual initialization of the mean model (blue contour) by clicking on prostate center, (c) Final segmentation result. Manual segmentation shown with green contour and the red contour show the segmentation achieved.

As stated before in Section 1, the robustness of the the proposed method against low SNR, intensity heterogeneities, shadow artifacts, speckle noise and micro calcification inside prostate is demonstrated in fig.4. As seen in fig.4(b) that on initialization a section of the mean model (blue contour) is located in a region of shadow artifact, the model successfully avoids the artifact and segments the prostate accurately with a DSC value of 0.94.

The mean model initialization in the TRUS images is done on visual inspection and therefore varies from one case to the other. Low standard deviation values of 0.01, 0.015 and 0.0001 associated with the DSC, specificity and sensitivity values seems to indicate that the final segmentation result of our method is not affected by the manual initialization of the mean model. To further validate our claim the standard deviation value of mean DSC over four independent test was computed and the mean of these values was 0.014. This further proves that accuracy of the process is indifferent to manual intialization. However, the mean model could be initialized automatically on the assumption that the prostate is visible in the center of the TRUS image. A more sophisticated approach would be an initial rough classification of the TRUS image to identify the prostate region and then initialize the mean model at the center of the prostate region.

Comparison of different prostate segmentation methodologies is difficult in absence of public datasets and standardized evaluation metrics, since the methods are developed with a wide variety of algorithms and with specific application requirements. However, to have an overall qualitative estimate of the functioning of our method we observe that the mean segmentation time of $0.72 \pm 0.05$ seconds for an image is comparable to [2](less than a second),[15](2.1 second), [11](5 seconds), [3](5 seconds) and inferior only to [20] that achieves segmentation time of $0.3sec$ in C++ and ITK framework. To have an estimate of overlap accuracy DSC value of $0.95 \pm 0.01$ is comparable to different measure of overlap accuracy value obtained by [12](Area difference 8.48%), [8](Area difference $4.79 \pm 0.68\%$), [10](Average similarity 89%), [18](Area overlap error $3.98 \pm 0.97\%$),[3](Area overlap $93 \pm 0.9\%$), [16](Area overlap 93%), [21](Area overlap 91%) and [4](Area accuracy 94.05%). MAD of our method of $1.48 \pm 0.36$ mm is comparable to [20](MAD $1.79 \pm 0.95$ mm), [12](MAD 2.61 mm), [13](MAD $4.4 \pm 1.8$ pixels), [9](MAD $2.79 \pm 1.94$ mm), [7]($6.21 \pm 4.03$ mm), and [11](Contour average distance $1.36 \pm 0.6$ mm). With reasonable conviction we can state that qualitatively our method performs well compared to some of the works in literature.

## 4    Conclusion

A novel approach of using Haar wavelet approximation coefficients to propagate AAMs with the goal of segmenting the prostate in 2D TRUS images have been proposed. Our approach is accurate, computationally efficient and robust to low SNR, intensity heterogeneity of prostate tisssue, shadow artifacts, speckle noise and micro calcification. It is observed that the use of the Haar wavelet approximation coefficients only, does not deteriorate the segmentation accuracy. While the proposed method is validated with prostate mid-gland images the effectiveness of the method against base and apical region slices is yet to be validated. Computational time of the process is fast but not suitable for real-time applications like MRI-TRUS fusion. We would like to explore the possibility of using the CUDA platform to achieve necessary hardware acceleration and parallelization in order to produce real time 2D segmentation of the prostate in TRUS images.

# Acknowledgements

This research has been funded by VALTEC 08-1-0039 of Generalitat de Catalunya, Spain and Conseil Régional de Bourgogne, France.

# References

1. Prostate Cancer Statistics - Key Facts (2009),
   http://info.cancerresearchuk.org/cancerstats/types/prostate
2. Abolmaesumi, P., Sirouspour, M.: Segmentation of Prostate Contours from Ultrasound Images. In: IEEE International Conference on Acoustics, Speech, and Signal Processing, vol. 3, pp. 517–520 (2004)
3. Betrouni, N., Vermandel, M., Pasquier, D., Maouche, S., Rousseau, J.: Segmentation of Abdominal Ultrasound Images of the Prostate Using A priori Information and an Adapted Noise Filter. Computerized Medical Imaging and Graphics 29, 43–51 (2005)
4. Chang, C.Y., Wu, Y.L., Tsai, Y.S.: Integrating the Validation Incremental Neural Network and Radial-Basis Function Neural Network for Segmenting Prostate in Ultrasound Images. In: Proceedings of the 9th International Conference on Hybrid Intelligent Systems, vol. 1, pp. 198–203 (2009)
5. Cootes, T.F., Hill, A., Taylor, C.J., Haslam, J.: The Use of Active Shape Model for Locating Structures in Medical Images. Image and Vision Computing 12, 355–366 (1994)
6. Cootes, T.F., Edwards, G., Taylor, C.: Active Appearance Models. In: Burkhardt, H., Neumann, B. (eds.) ECCV 1998. LNCS, vol. 1407, pp. 484–498. Springer, Heidelberg (1998)
7. Cosío, F.A., Davies, B.L.: Automated Prostate Recognition: A Key Process for Clinically Effective Robotic Prostatectomy. Medical and Biological Engineering and Computing 37, 236–243 (1999)
8. Ding, M., Chen, C., Wang, Y., Gyacskov, I., Fenster, A.: Prostate Segmentation in 3D US Images Using the Cardinal-Spline Based Discrete Dynamic Contour. In: Proceedings of SPIE Medical Imaging: Visualization, Image-Guided Procedures, and Display, vol. 5029, pp. 69–76 (2003)
9. Ding, M., Gyacskov, I., Yuan, X., Drangova, M., Downey, D., Fenster, A.: Slice-Based Prostate Segmentation in 3D US Images Using Continuity Constraint. In: 27th Annual International Conference of the Engineering in Medicine and Biology Society, pp. 662–665 (2006)
10. Ghanei, A., Soltanian-Zadeh, H., Ratkewicz, A., Yin, F.F.: A Three-Dimensional Deformable Model for Segmentation of Human Prostate from Ultrasound Images. Medical Physics 28, 2147–2153 (2001)
11. Gong, L., Pathak, S.D., Haynor, D.R., Cho, P.S., Kim, Y.: Parametric Shape Modeling Using Deformable Superellipses for Prostate Segmentation. IEEE Transactions on Medical Imaging 23, 340–349 (2004)
12. Knoll, C., Alcañiz, M., Monserrat, C., Grau, V., Juan, M.C.: Outlining of the Prostate Using Snakes with Shape Restrictions Based on the Wavelet Transform (doctoral thesis: Dissertation). Pattern Recognition 32, 1767–1781 (1999)
13. Ladak, H.M., Mao, F., Wang, Y., Downey, D.B., Steinman, D.A., Fenster, A.: Prostate Segmentation from 2D Ultrasound Images. In: Proceedings of the 22nd Annual International Conference of the IEEE Engineering in Medicine and Biology Society, vol. 4, pp. 3188–3191 (2000)

14. Larsen, R., Stegmann, M.B., Darkner, S., Forchhammer, S., Cootes, T.F., Ersbll, B.K.: Texture Enhanced Appearance Models. Computer Vision and Image Understanding 106, 20–30 (2007)
15. Liu, Y.J., Ng, W.S., Teo, M.Y., Lim, H.C.: Computerised Prostate Boundary Estimation of Ultrasound Images Using Radial Bas–Relief Method. Medical and Biology Engineering and Computing 35, 445–454 (1997)
16. Medina, R., Bravo, A., Windyga, P., Toro, J., Yan, P., Onik, G.: A 2D Active Appearance Model For Prostate Segmentation in Ultrasound Images. In: 27th Annual International Conference of the IEEE Engineering in Medicine and Biology Society, pp. 3363–3366 (2005)
17. Petrou, M., Sevilla, P.G.: Image Processing: Dealing With Texture, 1st edn. Wiley, Chichester (2006)
18. Shen, D., Zhan, Y., Davatzikos, C.: Segmentation of Prostate Boundaries from Ultrasound Images Using Statistical Shape Model. IEEE Transactions on Medical Imaging 22, 539–551 (2003)
19. Wolstenholme, C.B.H., Taylor, C.J.: Wavelet Compression of Active Appearance Models. In: Taylor, C., Colchester, A. (eds.) MICCAI 1999. LNCS, vol. 1679, pp. 544–554. Springer, Heidelberg (1999)
20. Yan, P., Xu, S., Turkbey, B., Kruecker, J.: Optimal Search Guided by Partial Active Shape Model for Prostate Segmentation in TRUS Images. In: Proceedings of the SPIE Medical Imaging: Visualization, Image-Guided Procedures, and Modeling, vol. 7261, pp. 72611G–72611G–11 (2009)
21. Zaim, A.: Automatic Segmentation of the Prostate from Ultrasound Data Using Feature-Based Self Organizing Map. In: Kalviainen, H., Parkkinen, J., Kaarna, A. (eds.) SCIA 2005. LNCS, vol. 3540, pp. 1259–1265. Springer, Heidelberg (2005)

# Novel Stochastic Framework for Accurate Segmentation of Prostate in Dynamic Contrast Enhanced MRI

Ahmad Firjany[1,4], Ahmed Elnakib[1], Ayman El-Baz[1,*], Georgy Gimel'farb[2], Mohamed Abo El-Ghar[3], and Adel Elmaghraby[4]

[1] Bioimaging Laboratory, Bioengineering Department, University of Louisville, Louisville, KY, USA
[2] Department of Computer Science, University of Auckland, Auckland, New Zealand
[3] Urology and Nrphrology Department, University of Mansoura, Mansoura, Egypt
[4] Department of Computer Engineering & Computer Science, University of Louisville, Louisville, KY, USA

**Abstract.** Prostate segmentation is an essential step in developing any non-invasive Computer-Assisted Diagnostic (CAD) system for the early diagnosis of prostate cancer using Dynamic Contrast Enhancement Magnetic Resonance Images (DCE-MRI). In this paper we propose a novel approach for segmenting the prostate region from DCE-MRI based on using a graph cut framework to optimize a new energy function consists of three descriptors: ($i$) $1^{st}$-order visual appearance descriptors of the DCE-MRI; ($ii$) a spatially invariant $2^{nd}$-order homogeneity descriptor, and ($iii$) a prostate shape descriptor. The shape prior is learned from a subset of co-aligned training images. The visual appearances are described with marginal gray level distributions obtained by separating their mixture over the image. The spatial interactions between the prostate pixels are modeled by a $2^{nd}$-order translation and rotation invariant Markov-Gibbs random field of object / background labels with analytically estimated potentials. Experiments with prostate DCE-MR images confirm robustness and accuracy of the proposed approach.

## 1   Introduction

Segmentation of the prostate is a basic task in many applications. It is a preliminary step in many Computer-Assisted Diagnosis (CAD) systems in detecting prostate cancer and calculating the prostate gland volume during biopsy. Although manual outlining of the prostate border enables the prostate volume to be determined, it is time consuming and subject to variability. Moreover, the traditional edge detectors are unable to extract the correct boundaries of the prostate since the gray-level distributions of the prostate and the surrounding organs are hardly distinguishable. Therefore, a number of investigations have

---

* Corresponding author. Tel.: (502)852-5092; Fax: (502)852-6806,
  aselba01@louisville.edu

A. Madabhushi et al. (Eds.): Prostate Cancer Imaging 2010, LNCS 6367, pp. 121–130, 2010.

been devoted to designing automatic or semi-automatic methods that are suitable for segmenting the prostate boundaries. These developed methods have been applied on different image modalities. The most common modality applied in the literature work on prostate segmentation is the transrectal ultrasound (TRUS) imaging [1,2,3,4], which is widely used for guided needle biopsy. However, magnetic resonance (MR) imaging has been recently suggested for improved visualization and localization of the prostate [5]. It provides valuable pathologic and anatomical information [5]. Moreover, new MR modalities, such as MR spectroscopy (MRS) and dynamic contrast enhanced MRI (DCE-MRI), have emerged as important tools for the early detection of prostate cancer. For these reasons, we will focus on the existing MRI prostate segmentation techniques.

Zwiggelaar et al. [6] have developed a segmentation technique based on polar-transform space and edge detection techniques. Zhu et al. [7] used a combination of an Active Shape Model (ASM) and 3D statistical shape modeling to segment the prostate. Toth et al. [8] presented an algorithm for the automatic segmentation of the prostate in multi-modal MRI. Their algorithm starts by isolating the region of interest (ROI) from MRS data. Then, an Active Shape Model (ASM) within the ROI is used to obtain the final segmentation. Klein et al. [9] has registered and matched an atlas training set of prostate images to the test image. The segmentation of the prostate is obtained as the average of the best-matched registered atlas set to the test image. Martin et al. [10] have presented a 3D method for segmenting the prostate. In this method, a probabilistic anatomical atlas was built and mapped to the test image. The resultant map is used to constrain a deformable model-based segmentation framework.

The major problem in the segmentation of the prostate is the exitance of a large variability in prostate appearance from patient to patient in intensity, texture, and size. In this paper, we present a general framework that takes into account all these issues. Our framework uses graph cuts to globally optimize a new energy function that accounts for the visual appearances of the prostate and the background, spatial interaction between their pixels, and the prostate shape. The prostate shape is learned from a subset of co-registered training images. The visual appearances are described with marginal gray level distributions obtained by separating their mixture over the image. The spatial interactions between the prostate pixels is modeled by a $2^{nd}$-order translation and rotation invariant Markov-Gibbs random field of object / background labels with analytically estimated potentials. We applied our framework in DCE-MRI as an emerging modality that offer the ability to distinguish benign from malignant tissues, which is our optimal goal after the segmentation step.

The paper is organized as follows: Section 2 overviews in brief our prostate segmentation based on a learned soft prostate shape model and an identifiable joint Markov-Gibbs random field (MGRF) model of DCE-MRI and "object–background" region maps. Experimental results are described in Section 3. Conclusions are presented in Section 4.

## 2 Segmentation of Prostate Using a Shape Model and a Joint MGRF Model of DCE-MRI

Let $\mathbf{Q} = \{0, \ldots, Q - 1\}$, $\mathbf{L} = \{\mathrm{ob}, \mathrm{bg}\}$, and $\mathbf{U} = [0, 1]$ be a set of $Q$ integer gray levels, a set of object ("ob") and background ("bg") labels, and a unit interval, respectively. Let a 2D arithmetic grid $\mathbf{R} = \{(x, y) : x = 0, 1, \ldots, X - 1; y = 0, 1, \ldots, Y - 1\}$ support grayscale DCE-MRI $\mathbf{g} : \mathbf{R} \to \mathbf{Q}$, their binary region maps $\mathbf{m} : \mathbf{R} \to \mathbf{L}$, and probabilistic shape model $\mathbf{s} : \mathbf{R} \to \mathbf{U}$. The shape model allows for registered (aligned) prostate DCE-MRI. The co-registered DCE-MRI and their region maps are modeled with a joint MGRF specified by a probability distribution

$$P(\mathbf{g}, \mathbf{s}, \mathbf{m}) = P(\mathbf{g}|\mathbf{m})P(\mathbf{s}|\mathbf{m})P(\mathbf{m}) \tag{1}$$

where $P(\mathbf{m})$ is an unconditional Gibbs distribution of co-registered region maps, $P(\mathbf{g}|\mathbf{m})$ is a conditional distribution of the DCE-MRI signals given the map, and $P(\mathbf{s}|\mathbf{m})$ is a conditional distribution of the prior shape of the prostate given the map.

As shown in Fig. 1, we focus on accurate identification of spatial interactions in $P(\mathbf{m})$, pixel-wise distributions of intensities in $P(\mathbf{g}|\mathbf{m})$, and prior distribution of the shape of the prostate in $P(\mathbf{s}|\mathbf{m})$ for co-aligned DCE-MR images. The probabilistic shape model $\mathbf{s}$ is learned from a training set of manually segmented and co-aligned images. To perform the initial prostate segmentation, every given DCE-MRI is aligned to one of the training images. The shape model provides the pixel-wise object and background probabilities being used, together with the conditional image intensity model $P(\mathbf{g}|\mathbf{m})$, to build an initial region map. The final segmentation is performed by optimizing the identified joint MGRF model of the DCE-MRI and region maps using a graph cut framework.

***Spatial interaction in the Prostate:*** A generic MGRF of region maps accounts only for pairwise interaction between each region label and its neighbors. Generally, the interaction structure and Gibbs potentials are arbitrary and can be identified from the training data. For simplicity, we restrict the interaction structure to the nearest pixels only (i.e., to the 8-neighborhood) and assume, by symmetry considerations, that the potentials depend only on the intra- or inter-region position of each pixel pair (i.e., whether the labels are equal or not) but are independent of its relative orientation. Under these restrictions, it is similar to the conventional auto-binomial (Potts) model and differs only in that the potentials are estimated analytically.

The 8-neighborhood has two types of symmetric pairwise interactions specified by the absolute distance $a$ between two pixels in the DCE-MRI slice ($a = 1$, and $\sqrt{2}$, respectively): (*i*) the closest pairs with the inter-pixel coordinate offsets $\mathbf{N}_1 = \{(\pm 1, 0), (0, \pm 1)\}$; and (*ii*) the farther diagonal pairs with the offsets $\mathbf{N}_{\sqrt{2}} = \{(1, \pm 1), (-1, \pm 1)\}$. The potentials of each type are bi-valued because only the coincidence of the labels is taken into account: $\mathbf{V}_a = \{V_{a,\mathrm{eq}}; V_{a,\mathrm{ne}}\}$

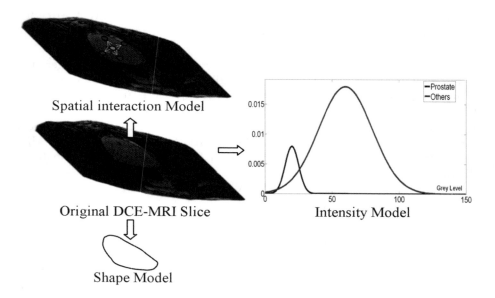

**Fig. 1.** Joint Markov-Gibbs random field model of DCE-MRI

where $V_{a,\text{eq}} = V_a(l, l')$ if $l = l'$ and $V_{a,\text{ne}} = V_a(l, l')$ if $l \neq l'$; $a \in \mathbf{A} = \{1, \sqrt{2}\}$. Then the MGRF model of region maps is as follows:

$$P(\mathbf{m}) \propto \exp \sum_{(x,y)\in\mathbf{R}} \sum_{a\in\mathbf{A}} \sum_{(\xi,\eta)\in\mathbf{N}_a} V_a(m_{x,y}, m_{x+\xi,y+\eta}) \qquad (2)$$

To identify the MGRF described in Eq.1, approximate analytical maximum likelihood estimates are formed in line with [12] as follows[1].

$$V_{a,\text{eq}} = -V_{a,\text{ne}} = 2\left(f_{a,\text{eq}}(\mathbf{m}) - \frac{1}{2}\right) \qquad (3)$$

where $f_{a,\text{eq}}(\mathbf{m})$ denotes the relative frequency of the equal label pairs in the equivalent pixel pairs $\{((x,y), (x+\xi, y+\eta)): (x,y) \in \mathbf{R}; (x+\xi, y+\eta) \in \mathbf{R}; (\xi, \eta) \in \mathbf{N}_a\}$.

***Conditional intensity model for DCE-MRI slice:*** We use a simple random field of conditionally independent intensities to model the DCE-MRI slice, given a region map:

$$P(\mathbf{g}|\mathbf{m}) = \prod_{(x,y)\in\mathbf{R}} p_{m_{x,y}}(g_{x,y})$$

---

[1] To the best of our knowledge, we are the first authors who introduced an analytical form to estimate Gibbs potentials.

where the pixel-wise probability distributions for the prostate and its background, $p_\lambda = [p_\lambda(q) : q \in \mathbf{Q}]$; $\lambda \in \mathbf{L}$, are estimated during the segmentation process. To separate $p_{\text{ob}}$ and $p_{\text{bg}}$, the mixed empirical distribution of all the pixel intensities is approximated with a linear combination of discrete Gaussians (LCDG)[2].

In this case the LCDG has two dominant positive DGs that represent modes associated with the object (i.e., prostate) and background, respectively, in the empirical intensity distribution for the DCE-MRI to be segmented. To approximate more closely this distribution, the LCDG also contains a number of positive and negative subordinate DGs:

$$p_{\text{LCDG}}(q) = \sum_{t=1}^{C_{\text{p}}} w_{\text{p},t} \psi(q|\theta_{\text{p},t}) - \sum_{t=1}^{C_{\text{n}}} w_{\text{n},t} \psi(q|\theta_{\text{n},t}) \qquad (4)$$

where the index $\alpha \in \{\text{p}, \text{n}\}$ specifies whether the DG is positive or negative, $C_\alpha$ is the number of such components, and $\theta_{\alpha,t}$ and $w_{\alpha,t}$ denote the weight and parameters of each individual DG $\Psi_{\theta_{\alpha,t}}$; $t = 1, \ldots, c_\alpha$, respectively. The LCDG of Eq. (4), including the numbers $C_{\text{p}}$ and $C_{\text{n}}$ of its components, is identified using our previous EM-based algorithm introduced in [11].

***Probabilistic model of the prostate shape:*** Most of the recent works on image segmentation use level set based representations of shapes: an individual shape is outlined by a set of boundary pixels at the zero level of a certain distance function, and a given shape is approximated with the closest linear combination of the training shapes. The main drawback of this representation is that the space of signed distances is not closed with respect to linear operations. As a result, linear combinations of the distance functions may relate to invalid or even physically impossible boundaries.

To circumvent this limitation, the probabilistic prostate shape model $\mathbf{s} : \mathbf{R} \rightarrow \mathbf{U}$ where $s(x,y)$ is the empirical probability that the pixel $(x,y)$ belongs to the prostate is learned from a training set of co-registered training DCE-MR images. The soft template is constructed as follows:

1. Co-align the training set of DCE-MRI using a rigid registration with mutual information as a similarity measure [13].
2. Manually segment the prostate from the aligned set.
3. Estimate the pixel-wise probabilities $s(x,y)$ by counting how many times the pixel $(x,y)$ was segmented as the prostate.

***Optimization of the Joint MGRF model using the graph-cut algorithm:*** After accurately identifying the joint MGRF model of the DCE-MRI image, the prostate segmentation problem turns to be a search for the Maximum A Posteriori (MAP) region map $\mathbf{m}$ in all the possible configurations of

---

[2] A discrete Gaussian (DG) $\Psi_\theta = (\psi(q|\theta) : q \in \mathbf{Q})$ with $\theta = (\mu, \sigma^2)$ is defined [11] as $\psi(q|\theta) = \Phi_\theta(q + 0.5) - \Phi_\theta(q - 0.5)$ for $q = 1, \ldots, Q - 2$, $\psi(0|\theta) = \Phi_\theta(0.5)$, $\psi(Q-1|\theta) = 1 - \Phi_\theta(Q - 1.5)$ where $\Phi_\theta(q)$ is the cumulative Gaussian function with the mean $\mu$ and the variance $\sigma^2$.

this joint MGRF model. The MAP region map is found by maximizing the interaction energy of the joint MGRF model. In this paper, we formulate a new energy function $E$ to accurately model the DCE-MRI image. This new function is formed as the logarithmic function of the probability distribution of the joint MGRF model given in Eq. 1:

$$E(\mathbf{m}) = \log(P(\mathbf{g}|\mathbf{m})) + \log(P(\mathbf{s}|\mathbf{m})) + \log(P(\mathbf{m})) \tag{5}$$

The search problem is an exhausting task and should be done in an efficient and precise way. We apply a graph-cut based algorithm (i.e., the $s/t$ Min-Cut/Max-Flow algorithm [14]) for such a task due to its powerful capability to end up with the optimal global region map [15]. As shown in Fig. 2, two-terminal graph-cuts with positive edge weights (maximizing the proposed energy $E$ in Eq. 5 using graph-cut is obtained by minimizing $-E$) are constructed as follow:

1. The first two terms in Eq. 5 define the object ($t$-links) by accounting for both the $1^{st}$-order visual appearance descriptors of the DCE-MRI and the prostate shape descriptor (i.e., $- \log(P(\mathbf{g}|\mathbf{m})) - \log(P(\mathbf{s}|\mathbf{m}))$).
2. The last term in Eq. 5 find the cuts ($n$-links) by penalizing for the spatially invariant $2^{nd}$-order homogeneity descriptor of the DCE-MRI (i.e., $- \log(P(\mathbf{m}))$).

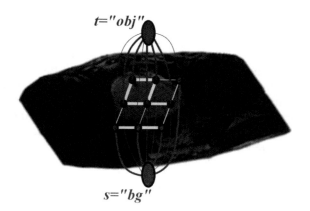

**Fig. 2.** Constructed two terminal graph-cuts: $t$-links (in blue and red) account for both the $1^{st}$-order visual appearance descriptors of the DCE-MRI and the prostate shape, and $n$-links (in light yellow) penalize for the spatially invariant $2^{nd}$-order homogeneity descriptor of the DCE-MRI (The thicker links donate greater affinity between corresponding nodes or terminals)

## 3   Experimental Results

We illustrate the performance of the proposed segmentation approach by applying it on 2D DCE-MRI prostate images. We observed that good selection of a

DCE-MRI imaging protocol is as important as the image analysis. The protocol described below has been found to be optimal with the current MRI hardware (Signa Horizon LX Echo speed; General Electric Medical Systems, Milwaukee, WI, USA). In our protocol, gradient-echo T1 imaging was employed by a Signa Horizon GE 1.5 Tesla MR scanner using an additional pelvic coil. Images were taken at 7 mm thickness with an interslice gap of 0.5 mm. The repetition time (TR) was 50 ms, the TE was minimum with flip angle at 60 degrees, the band width was 31.25 kHz, the field of view (FOV) was 28 cm, and the number of slices was 7. The DCE-MRI process started with a series of MRI scans which were used to establish a baseline in image intensity. These scans were performed without the administration of contrast enhancing agents so that the tissue's nonenhanced image intensity could be established. In the next stage, 10 cc of gadoteric acid (Dotarem 0.5 mmol/mL; Guerbet, France) was administered intravenously at a rate of 3 ml/sec. At this point, a series of MRI scans was performed every 10 seconds for 3 minutes, and every series contained 7 slices. To evaluate the classification accuracy, a radiologist manually segmented the "ground truth" for 98 different prostate images. These images represented 14 different series; each series contained 7 slices. Figure 3(a) shows some of the prostate images obtained using the above imaging protocol.

We divide the images into a training set and a testing set. The training set contains one third of the images and is used to provide the shape prior. The testing set contains two thirds of the images and is used to evaluate the performance of our segmentation approach. The segmentation separates the prostate object from the surrounding background. For comparison, the same images have been segmented using our proposed approach and the shape-based, level-set approach of Tsai et al. [16]. Figure 3 shows the comparative results for the testing prostate images with the known ground truth (manually segmented by radiologist). As shown in Table 1, differences between the mean errors for the two approaches are statistically significant by the unpaired $t$-test (the two-tailed $P$-values are less than 0.0001). To evaluate the selection of manually segmenting training images, we divide the data into three groups and performed the 3-fold cross validation. Table 2 shows that such a sensitivity is statistically insignificant.

**Table 1.** Accuracy of our proposed segmentation scheme on testing data in comparison to the level sets-based segmentation in [16]

|  | Algorithm | |
|---|---|---|
|  | Our | [16] |
| Minimum error, % | **3.3** | 4.96 |
| Maximum error, % | **8.8** | 50.9 |
| Mean error, % | **5.2** | 17.1 |
| Standard deviation,% | **1.2** | 17.4 |
| Significant difference, P-value | 0.0001 | |

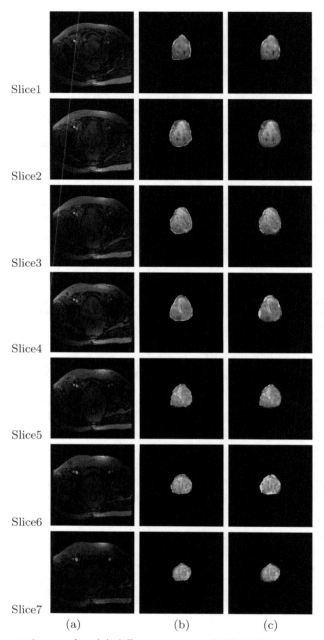

**Fig. 3.** Segmentation results: (a) different prostate DCE-MRI testing images, (b) our segmentation, and (c) segmentation with [16]. Error referenced to the ground truth (GT) is outlined in yellow (False Negative (FN): pixels segmented as the prostate in GT but not segmented as the prostate with our approach) and red (False Positive (FP): pixels segmented as the prostate with our approach but not segmented as the prostate in the GT)

**Table 2.** Sensitivity of the proposed approach to the training data using 3-fold cross validation

| | Tested Group | | |
|---|---|---|---|
| | Group A | Group B | Group C |
| Minimum error, % | 2.8 | 2.8 | 2.8 |
| Maximum error, % | 10.9 | 8.3 | 9.3 |
| Mean error, % | 4.9 | 4.7 | 5.1 |
| Standard deviation,% | 1.4 | 1.2 | 1.5 |
| Significant difference, P-value | (1,2):0.7491 | (2,3):0.7737 | (1,3):0.541 |

# 4   Conclusions

In total, we have presented a fully-automoted stochastic segmentation framework based on three image descriptors; the intensity gray level, the shape information, and the spatial information descriptors. These descriptors are embedded into a new energy function that is globally optimized using graph cuts. The results suggest that the proposed approach can precisely segment DCE-MRI prostate images. In addition, it is shown to be robust against their complex shape variations. The developed stochastic segmentation framework is very suitable to segment the anatomical structures that have noise and inhomogeneity problems. Therefore, it is not only useful for the medical imaging society but also for the computer vision applications. In our future work, we plan to extend the proposed 2D segmentation framework to include the segmentation of 3D prostate objects to quantitatively characterize the effectiveness and robustness of the proposed scheme.

# References

1. Shen, D., Zhan, Y., Davatzikos, C.: Segmentation of prostate boundaries from ultrasound images using statistical shape model. IEEE Transactions on Medical Imaging 22(4), 539–551 (2003)
2. Ladak, H.M., Mao, F., Wang, Y., Downey, D.B., Steinman, D.A., Fenster, A.: Prostate boundary segmentation from 2D ultrasound images. Medical physics 27, 1777–1788 (2000)
3. Zhan, Y., Shen, D.: Automated Segmentation of 3D US Prostate Images Using Statistical Texture- Based Matching Method. In: Ellis, R.E., Peters, T.M. (eds.) MICCAI 2003. LNCS, vol. 2878, pp. 688–696. Springer, Heidelberg (2003)
4. Gong, L., Pathak, S.D., Haynor, D.R., Cho, P.S., Kim, Y.: A Parametric Shape Modeling Using Deformable Superellipses for Prostate Segmentation. IEEE Transactions on Medical Imaging 23, 340–349 (2004)
5. Reynier, C., Troccaz, J., Fourneret, P., Dusserre, A., Gay-Jeune, C., Descotes, J.L., Bolla, M., Giraud, J.Y.: MRI/TRUS data fusion for prostate brachytherapy. Preliminary results. Medical Physics 31, 1568–1575 (2004)
6. Zwiggelaar, R., Zhu, Y., Williams, S., Zwiggelaar, R.: Semi-automatic segmentation of the prostate. In: Perales, F.J., Campilho, A.C., Pérez, N., Sanfeliu, A. (eds.) IbPRIA 2003. LNCS, vol. 2652, pp. 1108–1116. Springer, Heidelberg (2003)

7. Zhu, Y., Williams, S., Zwiggelaar, R.: Segmentation of volumetric prostate MRI datausing hybrid 2D+3D shape modeling. In: Proc. of Medical Image Understanding and Analysis, pp. 61–64 (2004)
8. Toth, R., Tiwari, P., Rosen, M., Kalyanpur, A., Pungavkar, S., Madabhushi, A.: A multi-modal prostate segmentation scheme by combining spectral clustering and active shape models. In: Reinhardt, J.M., Pluim, J.P.W. (eds.) Medical Imaging 2008: Image Processing. Proceedings of the SPIE, vol. 6914, p. 69144S (2008)
9. Klein, S., van der Heidi, U.A., Raaymakers, B.W., Kotte, A., Staring, M., Pluim, J.: Segmentation of the prostate in MR images by atlas matching. Biomedical Imaging: From Nano to Macro, 1300–1303 (April 2007)
10. Martin, S., Daanenc, V., Troccaz, J.: Automated segmentation of the prostate in 3D MR images using a probabilistic atlas and a spatially constrained deformable model. Medical physics 37, 1579–1590 (2010)
11. El-Baz, A., Gimel'farb, G.: EM Based Approximation of Empirical Distributions with Linear Combinations of Discrete Gaussians. In: Proc. IEEE Int. Conf. Image Processing, San Antonio, Texas, USA, September 16-19, pp. 373–376 (2007)
12. Farag, A., El-Baz, A., Gimelfarb, G.: Precise Segmentation of Multi-modal Images. IEEE Transactions on Image Processing 15(4), 952–968 (2006)
13. Viola, P., Wells, W.M.: Alignment by maximization of mutual information. In: Proc. 5th Int. Conf. Comp. Vision, pp. 16–23 (1995)
14. Boykov, Y., Kolmogorov, V.: An experimental comparison of min-cut/max-flowalgorithms for energy minimization in vision. IEEE Transactions on Pattern Analysis and Machine Intelligence 26(9), 1124–1137 (2004)
15. Boykov, Y., Funka-Lea, G.: Graph Cuts and Efficient N-D Image Segmentation. Int. J. Computer Vision 69(2), 109–131 (2006)
16. Tsai, A., Yezzi, A., Wells, W., Tempany, C., Tucker, D., Fan, A., Grimson, E., Willsky, A.: A shape-based approach to curve evolution for segmentation of medical imagery. IEEE Transactions Medical Imaging 22(2), 137–154 (2003)

# Boundary Delineation in Prostate Imaging Using Active Contour Segmentation Method with Interactively Defined Object Regions

Yan Zhang[1,*], Bogdan J. Matuszewski[1], Aymeric Histace[2],
Frédéric Precioso[2], Judith Kilgallon[3], and Christopher Moore[3]

[1] Applied Digital Signal and Image Processing Research Centre,
School of Computing Engineering and Physical Sciences,
University of Central Lancashire, Preston PR1 2HE, United Kingdom
[2] ETIS Lab, CNRS/ENSEA/Univ Cergy-Pontoise, 6, av. du Ponceau,
95014 Cergy-Pontoise, France
[3] North Western Medical Physics, The Christie NHS Foundation Trust,
Manchester, M20 4BX, United Kingdom

**Abstract.** Active contour methods are often methods of choice for demanding segmentation problems, yet segmentation of medical images with complex intensity patterns still remains a challenge for these methods. This paper proposes a method to incorporate interactively specified foreground/background regions into the active model framework while keeping the user interaction to the minimum. To achieve that, the proposed functional to be minimized includes a term to encourage active contour to separate the points close to the specified foreground region from the points close to the specified background region in terms of geodesic distance. The experiments on multi-modal prostate images demonstrate that the proposed method not only can achieve robust and accurate results, but also provides an efficient way to interactively improve the results.

**Keywords:** Image segmentation, prostate imaging, MRI, CT, TRUS, active contour, fast marching.

## 1 Introduction

Originally proposed in [1], active contour models for image segmentation have attracted extensive research in the past two decades. The basic idea of the active contour is to iteratively evolve an initial curve towards the boundaries of target objects driven by the combination of internal forces determined by the geometry of the evolving curve and the external forces induced from the image. Image segmentation method using active contour is usually based on minimizing a functional which is so defined that for curves close to the target boundaries it

---

* This work has been supported from the MEGURATH project (EPSRC project No. EP/D077540/1).

A. Madabhushi et al. (Eds.): Prostate Cancer Imaging 2010, LNCS 6367, pp. 131–142, 2010.

has small values. To solve the functional minimization problem, a corresponding partial differential equation (PDE) can be constructed as the Gateaux derivative gradient flow to steer the evolution of active contours.

The PDEs governing the evolution of active contours can be numerically approximated either by explicit or implicit methods. For explicit methods, an active contour is represented in a parametric form such as cubic B-spline [2]. The contour evolves as the parameters controlling the contour change. For implicit methods, also known as level set methods, an active contour is embedded as a constant level set in an embedding function (also called level set function) defined in a higher dimensional space. The evolution of the active contour is carried out implicitly by evolving its embedding function [3]. Thanks to level set's inherent capability to handle topological changes and straightforward extensibility to cope with high dimensional data, since the pioneering work in [4], level set based segmentation has motivated a large amount of methods. These methods not only explore a variety of image information [5,6,7,8,9], but also attempt to integrate static/statistical shape prior information into the framework [10,11].

Most existing active contour methods are focused on fully automatic segmentation. Once an initial contour is specified, users have no control over the evolution of the contour. If the result turns out to be unacceptable, the only things can be done by the users are either specifying another initial contour or tuning a few parameters related to the curve evolution algorithm. Then the users need to run the curve evolution again and wish the result could be better this time. This procedure is tedious and normally requires detailed knowledge of the segmentation method. Furthermore, there is no guarantee that a satisfactory result can be achieved. Due to these limitations, although active contour methods have found great success in some special areas, they are still of limited practical use in medical data segmentation. To change this situation, it is essential to introduce a user interaction mechanism into the active contour framework. In this paper, we propose an active contour method to allow users to specify foreground and background regions so that segmentation results can be progressively refined in a controllable way while keeping the user interaction to the minimum.

Prostate and surrounding organs segmentation is a demanding task due to the organs' close spatial proximity and changes in organs shape and appearance. Additionally depending on the imaging modality used, segmentation algorithm has to cope with a very low contrast and weak organ boundaries, complex textural patterns representing different organs or very high level of random and structured noise. Recently number of segmentation techniques have been proposed in literature aiming at semi-automatic prostate segmentation [12,13,14]. Most of these techniques do not allow, though, for interactive improvements of the segmentation, as the user interaction is limited to the algorithm initialization. Authors in [15] introduced such an interaction mechanism in their algorithm but it was based on, prior learn, statistical shape model of an organ of interest and image intensity information was not directly used in the algorithm. In this paper an algorithm similar, in guiding interaction principle, is proposed but contrary to [15] the algorithm directly uses the image intensity information.

## 2    Methodology

Let's denote the input image as $I$ and the specified foreground and background regions as $R_f$ and $R_b$ respectively. Let $S(p)$ represent an *open* curve with parameterization $p$ normalized in the range of $[0, 1]$, i.e., $S : [0, 1] \rightarrow \mathbf{R}^2 \in \Omega$ with $\Omega$ denoting the entire image domain. Then the geodesic distance function for the specified foreground region, denoted as $D_f(\mathbf{x})$, can be defined as

$$D_f(\mathbf{x}) = \inf_{S \in \mathcal{S}_f} \int_0^1 G(S(p); I) \cdot |S'(p)| \, dp \qquad (1)$$

where $\mathbf{x}$ denotes the coordinates of a point in the image domain and $\mathcal{S}_f$ represents the set of curves that connect the point $\mathbf{x}$ and the specified foreground region $R_f$, i.e., $\mathcal{S}_f = \{S : S(0) = \mathbf{x} \text{ and } S(1) \in R_f\}$. For an image with multiple channels, the geodesic metric $G(\mathbf{x}; I)$ is related to the smoothed gradient of each channel:

$$G(\mathbf{x}; I) = \sum_{i=1}^N |G_\sigma * \nabla I_i(\mathbf{x})| \qquad (2)$$

where $G_\sigma$ is the Gaussian function and $N$ is the number of channels. Similarly, the geodesic distance function for the specified background region, denoted as $D_b(\mathbf{x})$, can be defined as

$$D_b(\mathbf{x}) = \inf_{S \in \mathcal{S}_b} \int_0^1 G(S(p); I) \cdot |S'(p)| \, dp \qquad (3)$$

with $\mathcal{S}_b = \{S : S(0) = \mathbf{x} \text{ and } S(1) \in R_b\}$.

Since the geodesic metric $G(\mathbf{x}, I)$ is nonnegative, the geodesic distance functions can be calculated by solving the following eikonal equations with boundary conditions:

$$\begin{cases} |\nabla D_x(\mathbf{x})| = G_x(\mathbf{x}; I) \\ D_x(\mathbf{x}) = 0 \quad \text{for } \forall \mathbf{x} \in R_x \end{cases} \qquad (4)$$

where $x \in \{f, b\}$. Efficient approaches to numerically solve this type of equations can be found in [16,17].

Let $C(p)$ denote a *close* curve — a curve that divides the image domain into disjoint regions. Then, as illustrated in Fig. 1, the corresponding level set function $\phi(\mathbf{x})$ can be defined to satisfy the following conditions: (1) $C = \{\mathbf{x} : \phi(\mathbf{x}) = 0\}$; (2) $\phi(\mathbf{x}) > 0$ for $\mathbf{x}$ inside the contour and $\phi(\mathbf{x}) < 0$ for $\mathbf{x}$ outside. The normal of the active contour $\mathbf{N}$ is defined as the unit vector pointing to the direction that expands the contour. The proposed functional to be minimized is defined as

$$E(\phi(\mathbf{x})) = \int_\Omega D_f(\mathbf{x}) \cdot H(\phi(\mathbf{x})) \, d\mathbf{x} + \int_\Omega D_b(\mathbf{x}) \cdot (1 - H(\phi(\mathbf{x}))) \, d\mathbf{x}$$
$$+ \alpha \int_\Omega g(\mathbf{x}; I) \cdot |\nabla H(\phi(\mathbf{x}))| \, d\mathbf{x} \qquad (5)$$

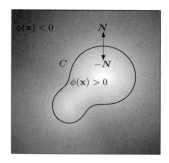

**Fig. 1.** Some conventions regarding active contour and level set applied in the paper

where $H(x)$ is the Heaviside function which equals to 1 when $x \geq 0$ and 0 otherwise. The functional consists of three terms. The first two terms indicate the fact that a good segmentation should separate pixels having small geodesic distances to the specified foreground region from those having small geodesic distances to the specified background region. The last term, weighted by a positive scalar $\alpha$, is from the geodesic active contour model [6] used for accurate location of object boundary, wherein $g(\mathbf{x}; I) = \exp(-\beta \cdot G(\mathbf{x}; I))$ with the positive scalar $\beta$ controlling the decreasing rate of the exponential function with respect to $G(\mathbf{x}; I)$.

By deriving the Gateaux derivative of the proposed functional, the implicit PDE, describing the evolution process of the level set function to achieve functional minimization, can be expressed as

$$\frac{\partial \phi(\mathbf{x}, t)}{\partial t} = (D_b(\mathbf{x}) - D_f(\mathbf{x}))|\nabla \phi(\mathbf{x}, t)|$$
$$+ \alpha \operatorname{div}\left(g(\mathbf{x}; I) \cdot \frac{\nabla \phi(\mathbf{x}, t)}{|\nabla \phi(\mathbf{x}, t)|}\right)|\nabla \phi(\mathbf{x}, t)|. \tag{6}$$

Note the introduction of time $t$ into the level set function to emphasize that it is an evolving process. Although the implicit PDE is practically used for level set implementation, its equivalent explicit PDE can reveal more insights into the evolution of the active contour itself. The equivalent explicit PDE can be written as

$$\frac{\partial C(p, t)}{\partial t} = (D_b(C(p, t)) - D_f(C(p, t))) \cdot \mathbf{N}$$
$$+\alpha \left(g(C(p, t); I) \cdot \kappa - <\nabla g(C(p, t); I), \mathbf{N}>\right) \cdot \mathbf{N} \tag{7}$$

where $\kappa$ is the curvature of the active contour and $< \cdot, \cdot >$ denotes the inner product of two vectors. The first term in the equation describes a region competition process. For every point on the active contour, there are two types of forces competing in opposite directions along the normal, namely, the contraction force exerted by $R_f$ and the expanding force exerted by $R_b$. The result of the competition depends on the geodesic distances between the specific point on the contour and the specified regions. It can also be seen that, for images with weak or ambiguous boundaries, $g(\mathbf{x}; I)$ can be set to constant 1, leading to the simplification of the second term to $\alpha\kappa\mathbf{N}$ which is a curvature flow used for curve smoothing.

## 3   Experimental Results

The objective of the first experiment is to demonstrate execution of the different stages of the proposed method. For this purpose bladder was selected as an object of interest (foreground) as it is an organ which is relatively easy to recognize and segment. The input MRI image with superimposed user selected regions is shown in Fig. 2(a). It can be seen that the regions can be defined by casual strokes with different labels, which reduces the efforts of user interaction. The geodesic metric computed using Equ. (2) is shown in Fig. 2(b) with intensity inverted for a better illustration of details. The geodesic distance functions associated with the bladder and non-bladder regions, as defined by the shown strokes, were computed using the fast marching method and are shown in Fig. 2(c) and Fig. 2(d) respectively. It can be seen that the functions increase as they propagate from their specified regions with sharp increase as they cross strong edges.

Fig. 3 shows a few iterations of the curve evolution process. To demonstrate the robustness of the method, the initial contours were chosen to be very dissimilar to the shape of the bladder. As shown in the first image in Fig. 3 these initial contours were defined as a set of uniformly spaced circles. As the algorithm progressed, the curves merged or vanished due to the level set's inherent ability to deal with topological changes. At the same time, the curves approached to the desired boundary due to the competition of geodesic distances induced from the bladder and non-bladder regions.

The second experiment was carried out to demonstrate another benefit of the proposed method — it is possible to improve segmentation results progressively. Fig. 4(a) shows the input MRI image with superimposed, region specifying, strokes, where different colors differentiate region labels and line widths differentiate regions selected in different stages of the segmentation process. Three user adjustments were performed. For the initial selection, specified regions, indicated by the bold strokes in Fig. 4(a), were used to get a rough segmentation as shown in Fig. 4(b). Based on this rough segmentation, more regions, indicated as median sized strokes, were added for the refined result shown in Fig. 4(c). Finally, more regions, indicated as the thin strokes, were added to get the final result shown in Fig. 4(d). The method is reasonably efficient, in terms of computational time, for interaction. For the image shown in Fig. 4(a) with size $240 \times 320$, the computation part of the process took about 0.8 second for each region adjustment on an Intel Quad CPU (Q6700) 2.66GHz within Matlab environment. In order to achieve efficiency, active contours were initialized as the boundary of $\{\mathbf{x} : D_f(\mathbf{x}) - D_b(\mathbf{x}) > 0\}$ to reduce the number of iterations. Additionally, AOS scheme [18] was applied to increase the time step for each iteration, without compromising the numerical stability of the algorithm.

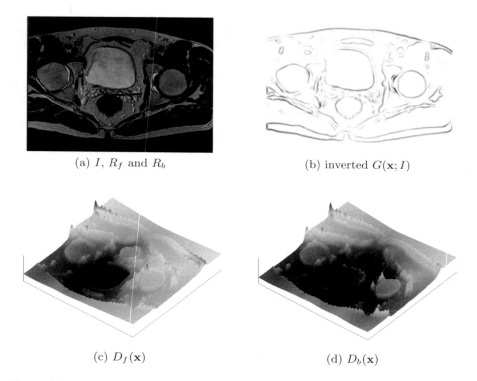

(a) $I$, $R_f$ and $R_b$          (b) inverted $G(\mathbf{x}; I)$

(c) $D_f(\mathbf{x})$          (d) $D_b(\mathbf{x})$

**Fig. 2.** (a) Original MRI image with superimposed specified foreground (red) and background (blue) region strokes; (b) Geodesic metric with intensity inverted; (c) and (d) Geodesic distance functions associated with the bladder and non-bladder regions respectively

Examples of the segmentation results for rectum, seminal vesicles and prostate delineated in an MRI data are shown in Fig. 5. It can be seen that even for the seminal vesicles, represented in the MRI by a complex textural pattern, an accurate segmentation can be obtained with only few approximate strokes.

The results obtained for organ segmentation from a CT data are shown in Fig. 6. In this case the method preformed well even though the segmented organs, represented by similar intensity patterns, are of low contrast with very weak edges between organs.

Fig. 7 shows segmentation result of the prostate from a transrectal ultrasound (TRUS) image [12]. Again the method preformed well despite a high level of noise, typical for this imaging modality. It should be stressed that for all the results shown in this section no image pre-processing was used. The method worked directly "out-of-the-box" with only active contour's smoothing parameter adjusted when segmenting different organs, though no changes were made to the method's design parameters when the same organ was segmented from different imaging modalities.

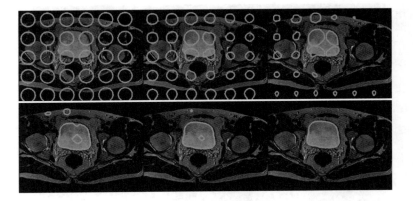

**Fig. 3.** A few iterations of active contour evolution with input strokes shown in Fig. 2(a). #iterations = 0, 2, 5, 10, 15, 20 from left to right and from top to bottom.

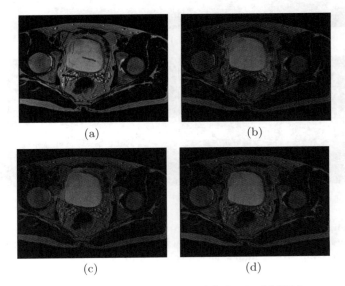

(a)                          (b)

(c)                          (d)

**Fig. 4.** Illustration of progressive segmentation. (a) Original MRI image superimposed with user specified regions (red for foreground and blue for background); (b) segmentation result from the first region selection with bold strokes in (a) as specified regions; (c) segmentation result from the second region adjustment with medium stokes in (a) as additional specified regions; (d) segmentation result from the third region adjustment with thin strokes in (a) as additional specified regions.

The method can also be used for segmentation of 3D data. A volumetric MRI scan, with manual prostate delineation approved by a clinician as ground truth, was used to test the algorithm. The MRI data consisted of 24 slices, among

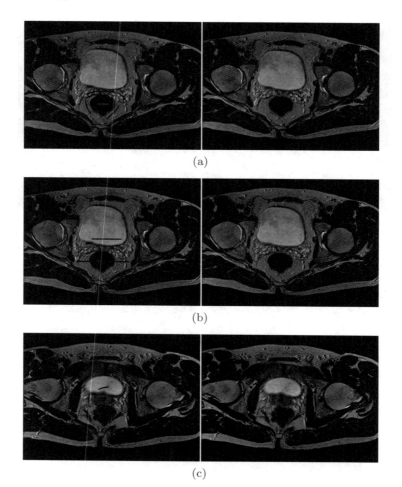

**Fig. 5.** Example of segmentation results from MRI data, with the strokes definitions shown in the left column and the corresponding segmentation results in the right column for (a) rectum, (b) seminal vesicles, (c) prostate.

which only three slices close to the top, bottom and middle of the data volume were selected and marked with specified regions as shown in Fig. 8. The whole region specification process, including slice selection, was done in less than a minute by one of the authors with very limited prostate delineation experience. Fig. 9 shows the segmented prostate as a red mesh in 3D and Fig. 10 shows a few image slices with corresponding contours, extracted from the segmented prostate surface, superimposed as the red curves. In both figures, the ground truth is indicated in blue for comparison. The segmentation error, defined as the percentage of absolute difference between the segmented and ground truth volumes over the ground truth volume, is around 8.52%.

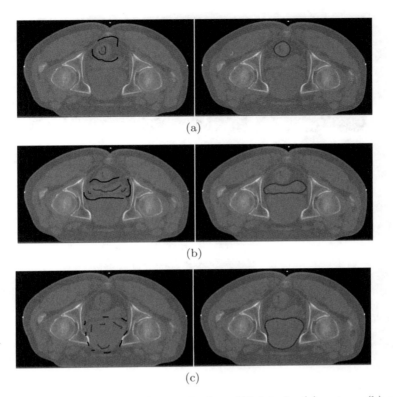

**Fig. 6.** Example of the segmentation results from CT data for (a) rectum, (b) seminal vesicles and (c) bladder

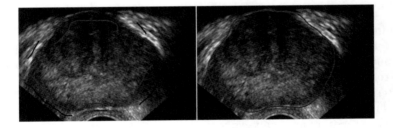

**Fig. 7.** Prostate segmented from the transrectal ultrasound image (the image was kindly provided by Prof. Ravi Sankar from the University of South Florida, Tampa, USA).

The paper does not contain a formal quantitative evaluation of the proposed method because due to the interactive nature of the method, obtained organs delineation will always reflect user subjective judgment and therefore a comparison of the segmentation results with the ground truth data would be effectively

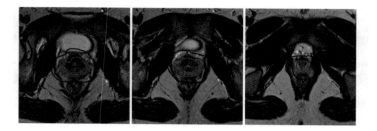

**Fig. 8.** Region selection on 3 slices of a volumetric MRI

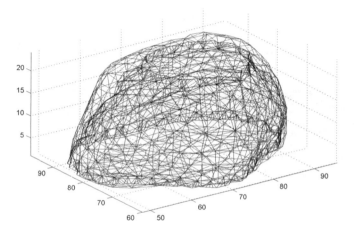

**Fig. 9.** Comparison of prostate results in 3D. Blue: from manual delineation. Red: from the proposed method.

testing inter- and/or intra- operator variability, thereby would not reflect on the method itself. Nevertheless further tests, investigating statistical dependence between number and length of region defining strokes and segmentation accuracy, are currently underway. In terms of the method efficiency, it took, for the results presented here, at most three and on many occasions just a single interaction to obtain the delineation which were considered to be accurate by an operator. The whole process of an organ segmentation on a tablet computer, for the shown 2D results, took on average just a few seconds. Segmentation of 3D data takes a bit longer as it is helpful when the region defining strokes are sparsely scattered across a volume occupied by the organ.

Overall, the authors believe that the proposed method provides good tradeoff between generalization properties of an automatic method and needs for clinician's subjective judgment.

Although for the sake of the presentation clarity a simple hybrid active contour model [19] was used it is straightforward to combine the proposed method with the most of existing active contour methods to equip them with the powerful

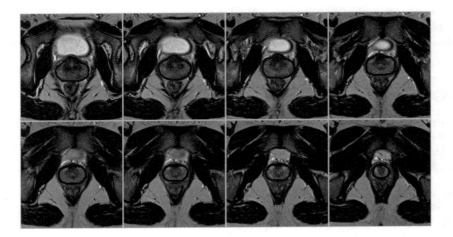

**Fig. 10.** Segmented prostate results on a few slices. Blue: from manual delineation. Red: from the proposed method.

tool of progressive refinement while keeping specific characteristics of the original method. Possible extensions can include active contour models incorporating a prior knowledge of the organ shape [11], topological constraints [20] or texture by which organ is represented in a given imaging modality [21]. With the help of Equ. (2) the method can be adopted for simultaneous organ segmentation in registered multiple-modality data.

## 4    Conclusions

The paper describes a novel segmentation method incorporating user specified regions into the active contour framework. The method can achieve robust results by evolving an active contour through competition of the forces induced by the specified regions and the input image providing an efficient way to refine segmentation results progressively. The method has been shown to be robust and able to cope with medical images of different modalities. More specifically it has been shown that the proposed method is an effective tool for segmentation of prostate and proximate organ at risk in imaging modalities typically used in diagnosis and treatment of prostate cancer patients.

## References

1. Kass, M., Witkin, A., Terzopoulos, D.: Snakes: Active contour models. IJCV 1, 321–331 (1988)
2. Precioso, F., Barlaud, M., Blu, T., Unser, M.: Robust Real-time Segmentation of Images and Videos Using a Smooth-Spline Snake-Based Algorithm. IEEE on Image Processing 14, 910–924 (2005)

3. Osher, S.J., Fedkiw, R.: Level Set Methods and Dynamic Implicit Surfaces. Springer, Heidelberg (2002)
4. Malladi, R., Sethian, J.A., Vemuri, B.C.: Shape Modeling with Front Propagation: A Level Set Approach. PAMI 17, 158–175 (1995)
5. Chan, T.F., Vese, L.A.: Active Contours Without Edges. IEEE on Image Processing 10, 266–277 (2001)
6. Caselles, V., Kimmel, R., Sapiro, G.: Geodesic Active Contours. IJCV 22, 61–79 (1997)
7. Cremers, D., Rousson, M., Deriche, R.: A Review of Statistical Approaches to Level Set Segmentation: Integrating Color, Texture, Motion and Shape. IJCV 72, 195–215 (2007)
8. Lankton, S., Tannenbaum, A.: Localizing Region-Based Active Contours. IEEE on Image Processing 17, 2029–2039 (2008)
9. Ni, K.Y., Bresson, X., Chan, T., Esedoglu, S.: Local Histogram Based Segmentation Using the Wasserstein Distance. IJCV 84, 97–111 (2009)
10. Munim, H.E.A., Farag, A.A.: Curve/Surface Representation and Evolution Using Vector Level Sets with Application to the Shape-Based Segmentation Problem. PAMI 29, 945–958 (2007)
11. Foulonneau, A., Charbonnier, P., Heitz, F.: Multi-reference Shape Priors for Active Contours Source. ICJV 81, 68–81 (2009)
12. Zhang, Y., Sankar, R., Qian, W.: Boundary Delineation in Transrectal Ultrasound Image for Prostate Cancer. Computers in Biology and Medicine 37, 1591–1599 (2007)
13. Vikal, S., Haker, S., Tempany, C., Fichtinger, G.: Prostate Contouring in MRI Guided Biopsy. In: MICCAI 2008 Prostate Workshop (2008)
14. Mahdavi, S.S., Salcudean, S.E., Morris, J., Spadinger, I.: 3D Prostate Segmentation in Ultrasound Images Using Image Deformation and Shape Fitting. In: MICCAI 2008 Prostate Workshop (2008)
15. Price, G., Moore, C.: Comparative Evaluation of a Novel 3D Segmentation Algorithm on In-Treatment Radiotherapy Cone Beam CT Images. In: Proceedings of the SPIE Conference on Medical Imaging, San Diego, USA, vol. 6512(3), pp. 38.1–38.11 (2007)
16. Sethian, J.A.: Level Set Methods and Fast Marching Methods. Cambridge University Press, Cambridge (1998)
17. Hassouna, M.S., Farag, A.A.: MultiStencils Fast Marching Methods: A Highly Accurate Solution to the Eikonal Equation on Cartesian Domains. PAMI 29, 1563–1574 (2007)
18. Weickert, J., Romeny, B.M.H., Viergever, M.A.: Efficient and Reliable Schemes for Nonlinear Diffusion Filtering. IEEE on Image Processing 7, 398–410 (1998)
19. Zhang, Y., Matuszewski, B.J., Shark, L.-K., Moore, C.: Medical Image Segmentation Using New Hybrid Level-Set Method. In: IEEE International Conference on Biomedical Visualisation, MEDi08VIS, London, July 9-11 (2008)
20. Zhang, Y., Matuszewski, B.J.: Multiphase Active Contour Segmentation Constrained by Evolving Medial Axes. In: IEEE International Conference on Image Processing, ICIP 2009, Cairo (2009)
21. Histace, A., Matuszewski, B.J., Zhang, Y.: Segmentation of Myocardial Boundaries in Tagged Cardiac MRI Using Active Contours: A Gradient-Based Approach Integrating Texture Analysis. International Journal of Biomedical Imaging (2009)

# Author Index

Printing: Mercedes-Druck, Berlin
Binding: Stein+Lehmann, Berlin